Learning to Walk by Faith:

Not by Assumption, But by the Spirit.

Author – Eld Joel Latimore Jr.

Learning to Walk by Faith: *Not by Assumption, But by the Spirit.*

Written by Eld Joel Latimore Jr.

© 2025 Eld Joel Latimore Jr.

Published by Latimore Publishing

ISBN (paperback): 979-8-218-82272-9

Scripture quotations are taken from the King James Version (KJV) of the Bible, unless otherwise noted.

Table of Contents

- Dedication

- Author's Note

- Preface

Dedication

To every believer who refuses to move on a hunch, to the weary who are learning to wait, and to the remnant who will not take a step until the Holy Ghost speaks or a true word from God is confirmed.

May your obedience become a testimony, and your testimony become a map for others.

— Elder Joel Latimore Jr.

Author's Note

This book was born from a simple conviction: faith is not assumption; faith is response to the Spirit **(Romans 10:17).**

In Scripture, the men and women of God did not guess His will—**they heard it,** whether by the Holy Ghost, by the Lord's direct appearing, or through a true prophet sent with His word. They moved only because God first spoke.

I am writing to help you recover that posture— listening before leaping—and to offer practical ways to *test, confirm, and obey* what the Spirit says.

You'll find throughout this book:

- **Scripture first.** The Word of God is our measure and guardrail.

- **Discernment in practice.** How to distinguish assumption, presumption, and true faith.

- **Witness and confirmation.** Honoring the Spirit's leading, the counsel of mature believers, and the fruit that follows obedience.

- **Reflection and action.** Each chapter ends with *reflective questions, reflective summary and a short prayer* to help you walk out what you've learned.

I do not write as a theorist but as a servant who has had to *wait, test, and obey*—often at great cost.

My prayer is that these pages will tune your ear to the Spirit and steady your feet for the path ahead.

—Elder Joel Latimore Jr.

Epigraph

21 And if thou say in thine heart, How shall we know the word which the Lord hath not spoken?

22 When a prophet speaketh in the name of the Lord, if the thing follow not, nor come to pass, that is the thing which the Lord hath not spoken, but the prophet hath spoken it presumptuously: thou shalt not be afraid of him.

— Deuteronomy 18:21–22 (KJV)

"My sheep hear My voice, and I know them, and they follow Me."

— John 10:27

Preface

Faith is not a feeling we upgrade to certainty. Faith is the human response to the voice of God—the Word *heard, believed, and obeyed.*

"Now faith is the substance of things hoped for, the evidence of things not seen" **(Hebrews 11:1).**

Substance and evidence do not come from our imagination; they come from God's self-disclosure.

Open the Scriptures and you will find a consistent pattern:

- **Noah** did not build an ark because the clouds looked strange—being warned by God, he prepared **(Hebrews 11:7).**

- **Abraham** did not wander on a whim—the LORD said, *"Go from your country..."* **(Genesis 12:1–4).**

- **Moses** did not challenge Pharaoh because he was bold—God called to him from the bush and sent him **(Exodus 3).**

- **Joshua** did not invent a battle plan—he received specific instruction about marching and shouting **(Joshua 6).**

- **David** inquired of the LORD again and again, *"Shall I go up?"* **(2 Samuel 5:19).**

- **Mary** did not assume favor—Gabriel brought a word from God **(Luke 1).**

The early church did not choose missionaries by talent—while they worshiped, the Holy Ghost said, *"Set apart Barnabas and Saul..."* **(Acts 13:2).**

In each case, *God initiates; people respond.* That is the grammar of faith.

By contrast, assumption wears religious clothing but lacks the breath of God. Israel presumed victory without the Lord's presence and fell **(Numbers 14:44–45).**

Saul spared what God said to destroy and called it worship **(1 Samuel 15)**.

The sons of Sceva borrowed language without relationship and were exposed **(Acts 19:13–16).** Presumption is noise; *faith is obedience.*

If our generation is to walk by faith, we must recover three holy commitments:

1. **Reverence for the Word.** Scripture is not a suggestion list; it is the living plumb line **(2 Timothy 3:16–17).** God will not contradict what He has written.

2. **Submission to the Spirit.** The same Spirit who inspired the Word illumines it and guides us **(John 16:13).** We learn His cadence through *prayer, repentance, and daily surrender.*

3. **Honor for true counsel**. God confirms His direction in community—through mature believers, proven prophetic voices, and the righteous fruit of decisions **(Proverbs 11:14; Matthew 7:16–20).**

This book invites you to slow down, listen deeply, and move when God speaks.

Expect practical guardrails: how to test impressions, how to wait without quitting, how to recognize confirmation, how to obey when obedience costs. *Expect encouragement through stories of faith in action—because obedience to God doesn't stop with one person; it becomes a signal of hope and direction for others. ".*

You may be standing at an edge right now— between comfort and calling, between fear and obedience. You don't need a louder world; you need a clearer Word. *The Shepherd still speaks. The Spirit still leads. The Father still delights to direct His children.*

Let us learn, together, **to walk by faith and not by sight**—*not by rumor, trend, or impulse,* but by the revealed will of God through *His Spirit* and *His Word*. And as we do, may our small obedience become mighty stories of His faithfulness.

But let us also be discerning. Not every voice that claims, *"God said,"* has truly heard from Him. Some pastors assume they are prophets when they are not. God gave the church the five-fold ministry—*apostles, prophets, evangelists, pastors, and teachers*—for a reason **(Ephesians 4:11–13).**

Each office carries *a unique grace, function, and responsibility.* To claim a role outside of God's calling is not only pride—it is dangerous. **This is not a game.** Souls hang in the balance, and the authority of the Spirit cannot be faked.

In these last days, false pastors and prophets abound—men and women who *assume, presume, and deceive,* speaking from their own imagination rather than from the Spirit of the Lord **(Jeremiah 23:16–17).**

Yet God still raises up true shepherds and prophetic voices who carry His burden faithfully. *Our task is to test every word, cling to what is good, and reject what is false.*

This book calls you to that higher standard: to test what you hear, to refuse empty noise, and to move only when God has truly spoken.

Come, Holy Ghost. Teach us to hear, and give us grace to obey.

— Elder Joel Latimore Jr.

Introduction

Faith is not a sprint we conquer in one leap; it is a walk we learn, *step by step,* with God. The Christian life is not built *on assumption, impulse, or personal ambition*—it is built on hearing the voice of the Spirit and obeying.

From **Genesis to Revelation**, every man and woman of faith moved only after God spoke. **Noah** built the ark because he was warned of things not yet seen. **Abraham** left his homeland because the Lord called him. **The disciples** followed Jesus because He said, *"Come, follow Me."*

None of them *assumed*. None of them *guessed*. None of them moved *on human reasoning*. They walked by faith because they first heard the voice of God.

Today, however, we live in a world that celebrates *noise, speed, and independence*. We are told *to trust our instincts, follow our feelings, and chase our dreams.*

But the Word of God gives us a different call: *"The just shall live by faith"* **(Romans 1:17)**. That faith is not rooted in ourselves—it is rooted in *God's Word, confirmed by His Spirit, and guarded by His truth.*

Tragically, many are being misled by *swindlers, charlatans, and false prophets* who speak in the name of the Lord but were never sent by Him.

Hardworking men and women are being bamboozled out of thousands of dollars, convinced they are sowing *"seeds of faith"* when in reality they are funding deception. Others are being led into dangerous acts in the name of God.

In Ohio, a 40-year-old Amish woman claimed she was *"testing her faith"* when she threw her 4-year-old son into a lake, *assuming* God had told her to. She was later charged with aggravated murder. Investigators reported that she insisted she was acting *"at the direction of God,"* but the tragedy revealed *deception and assumption,* not faith.

Hours earlier, her husband drowned during a similar so-called *"test of faith."* Even their other children were pressured into water-based trials, though they survived. This was not *Spirit-driven faith*—it was delusion, and it cost lives.

This book is not a collection of theories. It is a call back to true, **Holy Ghost, Spirit-driven faith**—the kind of faith revealed in Scripture that *listens before it leaps, tests before it moves, and obeys even when it costs.*

Such faith causes no harm to self or others, but always brings the fruit of God's Spirit: *guidance, peace, and life.*

My prayer is that as you read, the Holy Ghost will *tune your ears to His voice, sharpen your discernment, and steady your steps for the path ahead.*

In the chapters that follow, you will find:

- **Patterns from Scripture** that reveal how Spirit-driven faith begins.

- **Guardrails** to help you discern the Spirit and avoid presumption or false voices.

- **Practical steps** to grow stronger in hearing and obeying the Spirit.

- **Encouragement** to endure trials and keep walking faithfully when the road is hard.

This journey is not about learning techniques; it is about learning a Person—the Lord Jesus Christ, revealed to us in Scripture when rightly divided and by the Holy Ghost. He is *the Author and Finisher of our faith* **(Hebrews 12:2),** and He still leads His people today.

So, take a deep breath, quiet your heart, and open these pages with expectation. The Shepherd still speaks. The question is: will we follow?

A Prayer to Begin the Journey of Faith

Lord Jesus Christ,

I confess that I am a sinner in need of Your mercy. I have tried to live by my own strength and understanding, but today I choose to place my trust in You. I believe that You died on the cross for my sins and rose again with all power in Your hands.

Forgive me, cleanse me, and make me new. I turn away from sin and self, and I place my faith in You alone as my Savior and my Lord. Fill me with Your Holy Spirit, that I may hear Your voice, walk in obedience, and live the life of faith You have called me to.

From this day forward, I belong to You. Teach me to walk step by step with You, until I see You face to face.

In Jesus' name, Amen.

Chapter 1 The Call to Walk

"Before I formed thee in the belly I knew thee; and before thou camest forth out of the womb I sanctified thee, and I ordained thee a prophet unto the nations. " — **Jeremiah 1:5** (KJV)

Early Whispers (Mid-Sixties to 1979)

My faith journey did not begin in a chapel or during a revival service. It began in the mid-sixties, when I first heard the voice of God as a boy. I didn't know doctrine; I did not know Scripture. But I knew what I heard.

It wasn't thunder. It wasn't a dream. It was an explicit instruction in my spirit: *Stop. Don't do that—you'll regret it.* I obeyed. Then the voice went quiet. I wouldn't hear that same Voice again until decades later in Germany, when the Holy Ghost would arrest my life. But that first moment planted a seed: **God speaks—and if we listen, we live.**

As a youth, I was always told that I would be a preacher. Those who said it never told me how to become one. They never took me to church or introduced me to Jesus. I carried the image of myself preaching in my heart because that was how others saw me.

My father thought I would be a preacher because my birthday fell on the same date as Dr. Martin Luther King Jr. Others also identified something in me that I had not yet recognized in myself. But the truth was—*I didn't know Scripture, and most importantly, I did not know Jesus.*

I didn't know where to begin, or how someone like me could step into such a calling. I was left with an image, but no roadmap.

Deuteronomy emphasizes the importance of parents setting a good example for their children and raising them up in the Lord.

It is my believe that if we as a community of believers truly understood this and applied it to our families and communities, many of the problems we see in society today would be greatly reduced—if not eradicated.

In the early 1970s, my family and I moved from the Hough neighborhood to the Woodland Hills neighborhood. We lived off 93rd Street on Sophia Avenue, where I had many good friends but few good examples to follow.

My role models came mostly from television. I tried to imitate Robert Conrad, who played James West on the western series *The Wild Wild West,* thinking that was the kind of man to imitate. Only much later in life did I discover he was not.

Without a steady role model—or anyone truly watching over me—I had no guidance, no moral compass. I was drifting, learning life in all the wrong ways.

What I am emphasizing here is that children need good role models in their live to develop well.

I remember one time in particular when jealousy drove me where wisdom never would. A boy in the neighborhood had things I didn't—he had the kind of attention I craved.

Instead of being content with what I had, envy filled my heart. One day, that jealousy pushed me past the line. I didn't fight him. I didn't even confront him. I did something far worse: I broke into his home.

At the time, I thought I was getting even, proving myself, taking what I thought I deserved. But what I really proved was how lost I was.

Jealousy had become my teacher, sin my master. Looking back, I see it was not boldness but brokenness that drove me. I was a boy without guidance, a soul without an anchor, headed down a road that only God's grace could rescue me from.

An older boy in the neighborhood and I skipped school one day. With no plan and too much idle time, we wandered the block until temptation found us. *"Let's hit his house,"* the older boy whispered, pointing to the schoolmate we both secretly envied.

He was handsome, carried himself with confidence, and his afro was bigger than mine—a small thing, but in those days, hair meant status.

Envy is a petty master, and I was in the fifth or sixth grade, too young to know better but old enough to know it was wrong.

We slipped around to the back, our hearts pounding as we pried the basement window. It was the first time I had ever broken into anything, and the thrill of it mixed with fear in my chest.

We ransacked the place until we found a savings jar tucked away. Inside was fourteen dollars. Fourteen. That was all.

It felt like treasure in the moment. We stuffed it into our pockets and hurried out, trying to act casual as we walked back into the sunlight. On the outside, I tried to look tough, but on the inside, something was already gnawing at me.

I didn't have words then for *"conviction"* but I knew something wasn't right. Every time I thought about the boy, guilt tightened in my chest. I couldn't shake the thought that I had crossed a line I could never uncross.

Finally, the weight became too much. I confessed what I had done.

I blame my misguidance on the fact that I had no good role models in my life. And anytime a child does not have a good role model, he / she is apt to do anything just to get attention or feel wanted.

Not long after, judgment came looking for me. Word got around the neighborhood. Whispers spread. The embarrassment stung more than the fear of being caught. And I knew in that moment that the road I had stepped onto was dark, dangerous, and leading me nowhere good.

It was a turning point—not because I suddenly became righteous, but because I learned how empty sin really is. Fourteen dollars bought me nothing but shame.

That day taught me that jealousy takes more than it gives, and sin will always leave you with less than you had before.

The young man whose house we violated—and an older associate of his—caught me, pinned my back against a tree, and prepared to knock my teeth out because of what I had done.

As the older boy pressed me, I looked up over my right shoulder and saw—just for a second or two—a vision in the clouds: a large right leg extending out as if seated upon a throne.

It appeared, then slipped back into the clouds. I didn't understand it, but I knew something had shifted in that moment.

It was a sight too holy for me to put into words, yet it left me with the unshakable sense that a greater Power was present. The one who was ready to club me and knock my teeth down my throat… let me go.

Only later, much later, did I realize that God was showing me mercy before I even knew His name. Even then, He was watching, sparing, and teaching me that my life was not in my own hands.

I confided in my teacher and told her about the vision. I don't remember her response. But I remember the mercy.

At the time, I did not know the Scriptures. Later I would discover that the laws of Moses in **Exodus 22** required the **thief** to repay double the value of what was stolen if the item was found in his possession alive.

Without knowing any of that, I paid the young man back twice what I had stolen—not because I understood the Bible's language of *restitution,* but because something in me knew: *Make this right.* I still didn't know the word *repent*, yet God was already teaching me His ways.

For those who don't know, this is what I mean when I say: **Learning to Walk by Faith**—*Not by Assumption, but by the Spirit.*

By 1973, our family had moved from the Woodland Hills neighborhood to the Union/Miles community. I did not grow up in church. My mother, whom I love, raised me with *superstition and black magic.* I learned to fear *omens,* to watch for *"signs,"* and to try to bend the unseen to my will.

That mixture opened a dangerous door in my life. I drifted so far from the reality of God that I started to believe the oldest lie in the world: **I am my own god.** Pride felt like power.

In truth, it was a chain. Assumption told me I was in control, but the Spirit was quietly showing me I was bound.

As a result of this foolishness and false religion, I became mentally and spiritually confused about what was true and what was false. It showed— even in my appearance. I did not yet know my true identity as an elect child of God.

Before my conversion to Christ, I often visited *spiritual readers* who told me that I would one day be rich and that I needed to "watch out for the *strange woman.*" Their words sounded promising, but they planted a lie in me. Instead of pointing me toward *God's truth*, they fed my pride and twisted my focus.

I assumed wealth would come without labor, and that I could navigate relationships without God's guidance. They never told me how to avoid the *strange woman,* nor did they warn me that one day my own father would be instrumental in pushing me toward her.

What I didn't realize was that these so-called prophecies were bait—half-truths designed by the enemy to derail me before I ever learned to *listen to the Spirit.* Assumption said destiny could be handed to me by fortune tellers, but the Spirit was waiting to write His truth on my heart.

Because of those lies, I believed I didn't need to work hard in school or apply myself as other children did—that everything would simply fall into my lap.

Later, I learned that both they and I were wrong. It was all part of the devil's trap to keep me from discovering God's perfect plan for my life.

Elder's Wisdom: *Never expose a child—or anyone else—to the deception of the occult.*

Then, in 1979, I had a child out of wedlock. I was an uneducated hoodlum that did not know which way was up. Although I loved my baby's mother, we ended up separating.

Later on, in the year after our separation, the light broke through. I gave my life to the Lord Jesus Christ. This was the beginning of my faith walk. I didn't know Him well, but He knew me, and I knew I needed Him.

I began to share my faith with my mother, my father, and my siblings. These were the same people who once told me I would be a preacher.

So, it should not have shocked them when I got saved—yet most of them doubted rather than believed. Perhaps they too were still caught under the same deception of believing they were their own gods.

Still, I was a newborn trying to run. I wasn't yet fully loyal to the Lord or to what my pastor was asking of me. I had *sincerity* without surrender, *zeal* without depth. I could talk about Him, but I did not yet walk with Him daily.

Looking back, I see the pattern. God had been speaking—through a warning as a child, through conviction after sin, through a vision that spared me from violence, through the pull toward restitution—long before I had words for any of it.

He was shepherding a stubborn heart toward Himself. I didn't yet know the Lord, but the Lord already knew me.

That moment in 1979—when I surrendered my life to the Lord—wasn't the end of the journey. It was only the beginning.

I can still see that day in my mind. The church was nothing grand—a small storefront on Superior Avenue in East Cleveland.

The pastor invited everyone to the altar for prayer. I stayed behind, arms crossed, watching.

People were shouting, dancing, speaking in tongues. To me it looked like chaos. My first thought was, *Phony baloney*. They're just putting on a show. I could get up there and do the same thing.

So, I tested it. I walked up to the altar with my own plan, ready to prove the whole thing was fake. I started moving my feet, mimicking what I saw. But then something I never expected happened—*I couldn't stop.*

What began as mockery became mystery. I
looked down, and it felt as if my feet weren't
even touching the floor.

A presence I couldn't explain had taken over.
Even while I mocked, He loved me. Even while I
tested Him, He was proving Himself faithful.

In that instant, my argument lost its power. What
I had dismissed as noise and pretense was in fact
something real—something holy. I didn't
understand it, but I knew I had stepped into the
presence of God.

I had no blueprint, no strong knowledge of the
Scriptures, no long church background. All I had
was a stirring in my heart that could only have
come from the Spirit of God. And that was
enough to change me.

During this season, I also found a man I could look up to—my pastor, **Elder Larry Jackson**. I wanted to preach like him, quote scriptures like him, I wanted to dance in the aisles like him.

To me, he represented what a man of God looked like—or so I thought. Looking back now, I see that *this was my first step in learning what it truly means to walk by faith—not by assumption, but by the Spirit.*

I didn't choose Christ because it was popular. I didn't surrender because it made sense to my natural mind. I responded to an inner pull that I couldn't explain, yet I couldn't deny. *That is faith at its earliest stage: not assumption, but response.*

Faith does not require us to see the entire path—
it requires us to trust the One who calls us
forward. When I gave my life to Jesus, I had
more questions than answers. I was immature,
untrained, and still entangled in many things I
would later have to lay down.

But obedience, even in its smallest measure,
became the seed that God could water. That first
"yes" was clumsy, but it was real—and God
honors even the weakest step when it is a step
toward Him.

Reflective Questions:

1. Have you ever heard God's voice—
   through conviction, mercy, or warning—
   even before you knew who He was? How
   did you respond?

2. In your youth, who (or what) shaped your
   understanding of identity and purpose?
   Were they godly influences or worldly
   ones?

3. What false beliefs, superstitions, or lies did
   you once cling to that God has since
   exposed as chains?

4. When you look back over your life, can you see God's hand guiding you—even in moments when you didn't recognize Him?

5. What is holding you back right now from fully surrendering to Jesus Christ and trusting Him to lead your life?

Reflective Summary:

Chapter 1 reminds us that the call of God often begins before we truly understand it.

For me, it was a whisper in the sixties, a vision in the clouds, and a stirring in my heart long before I had the language of Scripture.

I didn't know *doctrine,* I didn't know *church,* and I didn't even know *Jesus personally*—but God knew me.

His mercy spared me when I deserved judgment. His Spirit pushed me toward *restitution* when I only knew guilt. His voice kept calling me until, in 1979, the light broke through and I surrendered.

Faith, at its core, *is not assumption but response. It is not built on popularity, ritual, or family tradition.*

It is answering the inner pull of the Spirit with a trembling but willing **"yes."** That first step may be clumsy, but it is real—and God honors even the smallest act of obedience when it is directed toward Him.

Initial Prayer of Faith and Deliverance (Romans 10:9–13):

"That if thou shalt confess with thy mouth the Lord Jesus, and shalt believe in thine heart that God hath raised him from the dead, thou shalt be saved.

For with the heart man believeth unto righteousness; and with the mouth confession is made unto salvation.

For the scripture saith, *Whosoever believeth on him shall not be ashamed... For whosoever shall call upon the name of the Lord shall be saved."*

(Romans 10:9–11, 13)

Prayer:

Heavenly Father,

I come to You today acknowledging my sins and the lies I once believed. I confess that I have tried to live life my own way, and I repent for every time I thought I could be my own god.

Lord Jesus, I believe that You died for my sins and that God raised You from the dead.

I confess with my mouth that You are Lord of my life, and I invite You into my heart right now.

Wash me with Your blood, deliver me from deception, and fill me with Your Spirit.

By faith, I receive salvation, forgiveness, and a new beginning. Thank You, Lord, for hearing me—for according to Your Word, whoever calls on Your name shall be saved.

In Jesus' name, Amen.

"And in this season, I was Learning to Walk by Faith: Not by Assumption, But by the Spirit."

Chapter 2: From Call to Completion

"Moreover whom he did predestinate, them he also called: and whom he called, them he also justified: and whom he justified, them he also glorified."

— Romans 8:30 (KJV)

The salvation of a soul is not an accident, nor is it merely the result of human effort. It is the work of God from beginning to end — from the first whisper of His call to the final moment when we stand glorified in His presence.

Salvation is not random, fragile, or unfinished. It is the eternal plan of God unfolding in time, carried out by His Spirit, applied to His people.

This journey can be understood in stages: *effectual calling, conversion* (repentance and faith), *regeneration, justification, adoption, sanctification, and glorification.*

Together, they form the golden chain of salvation — each link forged by the hand of God, unbreakable, unshakeable, and certain to reach its destination.

Effectual Calling

The doctrine of salvation begins not with man, but with God. Before repentance can rise in the heart or faith can take root in the soul, God must first act. This is what Scripture calls His effectual calling.

There is a general call of the gospel — the open invitation to all: *"Come unto me, all ye that labour and are heavy laden, and I will give you rest"* **(Matthew 11:28).**

But there is also a deeper, inward call, aimed at those whom God has chosen. Jesus Himself explained, *"Many are called, but few are chosen"* **(Matthew 22:14).**

The general call can be resisted, ignored, or rejected. **The effectual call**, however, accomplishes its purpose. The Spirit moves within a person's heart, opening their eyes, stirring conviction, and making Christ irresistible.

For Saul of Tarsus, it came as a blinding light on the Damascus Road **(Acts 9).**

For Lydia in Philippi, it was as gentle as the Lord opening her heart to receive Paul's words **(Acts 16:14).**

Whether dramatic or quiet, the effectual call brings the same result: the sinner is summoned, and the sinner comes.

Conversion: Repentance and Faith

When God calls, the sinner responds through conversion — a turning away from sin and a turning toward God.

1. Repentance

Repentance is more than feeling bad about wrongdoing. It is a Spirit-produced change of mind, heart, and direction.

To repent is to agree with God about *sin, grieve over it, and forsake it.* The Thessalonians modeled this when they *"turned to God from idols to serve the living and true God"* **(1 Thessalonians 1:9).**

Repentance without faith leads only to despair. **Faith** without repentance produces false assurance. Both are inseparably joined in true conversion.

2. Faith

Faith is the other side of conversion. If repentance is the hand that releases sin, faith is the hand that clings to Christ.

Faith is more than intellectual agreement with facts about Jesus. It is entrusting yourself fully to Him — resting the weight of your soul on His death and resurrection.

Paul reminds us, *"For by grace are ye saved through faith; and that not of yourselves: it is the gift of God"* **(Ephesians 2:8).**

True faith involves:

- Knowledge of God's truth,

- Assent that the truth is real, and

- Trust that Christ is sufficient to save.

Faith is not a one-time act; it is a daily reliance. **As Scripture declares:** *"The just shall live by faith"* **(Romans 1:17).**

Regeneration

Beneath repentance and faith lies the hidden miracle of regeneration — the new birth.

Jesus told Nicodemus, *"Except a man be born again, he cannot see the kingdom of God"* **(John 3:3).**

Regeneration is not moral reform, nor self-discipline, nor education. It is the Spirit of God breathing life into the spiritually dead.

Titus 3:5 describes it this way: *"Not by works of righteousness which we have done, but according to his mercy he saved us, by the washing of regeneration, and renewing of the Holy Ghost."*

In regeneration, the heart of stone becomes a heart of flesh **(Ezekiel 36:26).**

A new set of desires emerges: once we loved darkness, now we crave the light. **Regeneration** explains why God's call cannot fail — because He gives new life to answer His own summons.

Justification and Adoption

The inward change of regeneration is accompanied by outward declarations from God Himself.

Justification is God's legal verdict: the sinner is declared righteous on the basis of Christ's finished work. *"Therefore being justified by faith, we have peace with God through our Lord Jesus Christ"* **(Romans 5:1).**

Our guilt is removed, and Christ's righteousness is credited to our account.

Adoption goes even further. God does not merely declare us "not guilty"; He receives us as His children. *"Behold, what manner of love the Father hath bestowed upon us, that we should be called the sons of God"* **(1 John 3:1).**

Through the Spirit of adoption, we cry, *"Abba, Father"* **(Romans 8:15).**

Together, justification secures our standing, and adoption secures our belonging. We are not only acquitted criminals but beloved children.

Sanctification

Salvation does not end at conversion. The same Spirit who *called, regenerated, and justified* us continues His work in **sanctification.**

Sanctification is the process of being made holy — set apart for God's purposes. Positionally, we are already holy in Christ. Practically, we are being made holy day by day.

This is a partnership: *"Work out your own salvation with fear and trembling, for it is God which worketh in you both to will and to do of his good pleasure"* **(Philippians 2:12–13).**

Sanctification is often slow, marked by discipline, struggle, and steady growth. The fruit of the Spirit — *love, joy, peace, patience, kindness, goodness, faithfulness, gentleness, and self-control* **(Galatians 5:22–23)** — becomes increasingly evident as Christ's character is formed in us.

It is not perfection in this life, but **transformation.** Every small victory over sin, every act of obedience, every renewed desire for God testifies that the Spirit is at work.

Glorification

The story of salvation ends not in struggle, but in triumph. **Glorification** is the final act of **redemption,** when every trace of sin will be removed and every believer will be conformed fully to Christ.

"When Christ, who is our life, shall appear, then shall ye also appear with him in glory" **(Colossians 3:4).**

On that day, the mortal will put on immortality, sorrow will give way to joy, and faith will give way to sight. The journey that began with God's call will end with eternal glory.

The Journey in Between

It is important to remember that **salvation** is not always experienced like Paul's Damascus Road encounter. Some are drawn quickly, others slowly. For many, the Christian life unfolds through years of *trial, discipline, setbacks, and growth.*

Salvation is not a sprint but a marathon. Some begin with fire and passion; others stumble forward with weakness and tears. But the same grace that called us will carry us.

Paul reassures us: *"Being confident of this very thing, that he which hath begun a good work in you will perform it until the day of Jesus Christ"* **(Philippians 1:6).**

The chain of salvation is unbreakable because every link is held by God Himself. From call to completion, He is faithful.

Our task is to endure, to keep walking by faith, and to trust that the One who started the work will finish it.

Reflective Questions:

1. How does understanding God's effectual calling change the way you view your salvation?

2. In your own walk, have you experienced repentance and faith as two sides of the same coin? How so?

3. Which of the salvation truths — justification, adoption, sanctification, or glorification — brings you the most comfort right now, and why?

4. Where do you see the evidence of sanctification in your life today? In what areas do you still need the Spirit's refining work?

5. How does the assurance that "He who began a good work will complete it" (Philippians 1:6) help you endure struggles and setbacks in your journey of faith?

Reflective Summary:

Salvation is not merely a momentary decision but a lifelong process authored and completed by God Himself.

From His effectual call to our final glorification, the believer's journey rests in His hands.

Repentance and faith mark the beginning, regeneration provides the new life, justification secures our standing, adoption gives us belonging, sanctification shapes us daily, and glorification assures us of a glorious end.

This chapter reminds us that salvation is a chain unbroken by human weakness. Even when our steps falter, God's plan marches forward.

He is not only the Author but also the Finisher of our faith. Our role is to endure, to trust, and to keep walking with the confidence that what He has begun, He will surely complete.

Prayer

Heavenly Father,

I thank You for calling me out of darkness into
Your marvelous light. Thank You for the gift of
repentance, the grace of faith, the miracle of
regeneration, and the security of justification and
adoption. Continue to sanctify me by Your Spirit
and conform me daily to the image of Christ.

Lord, when I grow weary, remind me that You
are faithful to complete what You have begun.
Help me to endure with patience, walk in
holiness, and keep my eyes fixed on the hope of
glory.

In Jesus' name, Amen.

Chapter 3 Early Steps: Zeal Without Depth

But he that received the seed into stony places, the same is he that heareth the word, and anon with joy receiveth it; yet hath he not root in himself, but dureth for a while: for when tribulation or persecution ariseth because of the word, by and by he is offended.

—Matthew 13:20–21 (KJV)

The first step of surrender in 1979 opened the door to my faith walk, but it did not make me a mature believer overnight. I was excited about being saved—I wanted to tell everyone, especially my family.

I shared my new faith with my mother, my father, and my siblings. But though my words were bold, my roots were still shallow.

Like many new believers, I mistook enthusiasm for maturity. I had the language of salvation, but I lacked the discipline of discipleship.

I could testify about Jesus on Sunday, yet still struggle to follow Him on Monday. I had *sincerity* without surrender, *zeal* without depth. My heart was turned toward the Lord, but my habits were still entangled with the world.

This was a season of learning that faith is more than a feeling. It is more than excitement. It is a daily decision to walk with God—even when the newness wears off, even when obedience costs something. And because I had not yet learned that lesson, I stumbled often.

Later in 1979, I met a young lady, whom I will call Jo. Of course, Jo is not her real name. However, I assumed that because her name was similar to mine, and we were about the same age, that she was my soulmate.

She was smart, though not as sharp as Pat—the woman who had my first child. Looking back, Pat should have been my wife. But because of my ignorance, I ruined that relationship. She left me because of a terrible lie I repeated—a lie my parents told me to tell her—that the baby she was carrying was not mine.

That deception was the devil's work, a consequence of not having Christ in the home or in the heart and no true moral compass.

I honestly don't know what my parents expected of me; they never said. I wanted to grow and mature, but without true moral guidance, I saw myself heading in the wrong direction.

By 1981, Jo became pregnant. I didn't want to lose her, but in the end, I lost both her and the baby in a painful way.

For reasons I still don't fully understand, my father and mother did not want me to marry Jo.

I didn't know how to go about marrying her on my own, and no one seemed willing to help me.

We tried to marry on our own but to no avail.

My father had it in his mind that I would one day marry a white woman. Not a particular woman— just the idea of one. And sadly, I did end up marrying a white woman later, not because it was God's will, but because of my father's influence. That marriage became my downfall. It turned out to be the strange woman.

I remember visiting Jo one day at her home before the baby was born in her early stage of pregnancy. While we were talking about marriage, she suddenly slipped into what I can only describe as a trance. It was as if she were prophesying or a spirit speaking through her. She said, *"They say you are not going to marry me; that you are going to marry a strange woman."*

I told her, *"No, I will marry you. I'll get my father and mother to help me."*

She shook her head and said, *"They say, your father and mother won't help you marry me. And if you don't marry me, I am going to be a no-good woman."*

Then she added something that shook me: *"They say that you are going to be a powerful man."*

I laughed it off and asked, *"What am I going to be—the President?"*

She answered, *"No. More powerful than the President."*

Her words stayed with me. I tried to get my parents to help me marry her, hoping to avoid the outcome she had spoken of. But just like she said, they refused.

Looking back, I realize I could have been spared so much pain and hardship if only my parents had listened.

In time, Jo's mother moved from Cleveland to Rochester, New York.

After the baby was born, Jo—already weary from the pressure she carried—moved to Rochester as well. Just like that, she and the baby were gone from my life.

I was left standing in the ruins of my own choices, torn between the zeal of a new believer and the weight of old habits and family influence.

My words were bold, but my roots were still shallow. My heart burned for God, yet I lacked the wisdom to walk faithfully.

Looking back, I see how Scripture was already being lived out in me: *"he hath not root in himself, but dureth for a while."* I had sincerity without *surrender*, passion without *depth*. God was trying to shape me, but I was still too entangled in the world to fully yield.

For those who don't know, this is what I mean when I speak of **Learning to Walk by Faith: Not by Assumption, But by the Spirit.**

At that stage of my life, I was full of assumption—assuming Jo was my soulmate because of her name and because the love we had for each other, assuming my parents would help me, assuming zeal was enough to carry me. But I was not yet walking by the Spirit.

What happened next would teach me that zeal, by itself, cannot keep you. Only the Spirit can.

Reflective Questions:

1. Have I ever confused spiritual enthusiasm with true spiritual maturity? In what ways?

2. What habits or influences from my past are still entangling me and keeping me from growing deeper in Christ?

3. How do I respond when God's will conflict with my family's expectations or cultural pressures?

4. When I look back on my early faith, do I see areas where I was walking by assumption rather than by the Spirit?

5. What practical steps can I take today to ensure that my zeal is rooted in discipline, obedience, and surrender to the Holy Spirit?

Reflective Summary

Chapter 3 reminds us that zeal alone cannot sustain a believer. Like seed planted on stony ground, enthusiasm without depth quickly withers when trials come.

God desires more than excitement; He calls us to daily surrender.

Joel's story with Pat, Jo, and the influence of his parents illustrates the danger of mistaking passion for maturity and assumption for faith.

The call is clear: walking with God requires roots, not just leaves. True discipleship is not found in our emotions, but in our obedience to the Spirit.

Prayer

Heavenly Father,

I thank You for the gift of salvation and for the zeal that comes with knowing You.

But Lord, I do not want to remain shallow in my walk. Teach me to move from mere enthusiasm to true discipleship.

Uproot assumptions in my life and plant me deeply in the truth of Your Word.

Give me the wisdom to discern Your Spirit's leading, even when it costs me something, even when others do not understand.

Strengthen me so that I will not stumble under pressure, but stand firm in Christ. Lord, I ask You to mature me *in faith, in wisdom, and in obedience.*

Let my zeal be anchored in Your Spirit and not in my flesh.

In Jesus' name, Amen.

"And in this season, I was Learning to Walk by Faith: Not by Assumption, But by the Spirit."

Chapter 4 No Direction, Only Assumptions

There is a way which seemeth right unto a man, but the end thereof are the ways of death.

—Proverbs 14:12 (KJV)

By 1981, my life was unraveling. Pat and the baby had moved on, marrying someone enlisted in the U.S. Air Force. My other baby's mother, Jo had relocated to Rochester, and I was sinking deeper into unfaithfulness, without guidance, without a moral compass and without a role model.

I tried to keep in touch with Jo through phone calls, but the distance only widened the gap. The truth is, I was terrible. I had not realized it yet, but I needed Jesus more than ever, but instead of surrendering, I wandered.

It was also a time of uncertainty in America. The economy was shaky, and Ronald Reagan had just taken office with an agenda to strengthen the U.S. military. Around me, several of my buddies were signing up—finding structure, direction, and a steady paycheck in uniform.

Meanwhile, I was twenty-one years old and still in high school—a clear sign of how lost I had become and how fragile the structure of my family life really was.

I felt overlooked and ignored, as though my mother and father were more concerned with their own affairs than with what was happening to me. With no guidance, no affirmation of manhood, and no role model to look up to, I drifted further.

I had stumbled, wasted time, and let life slip past me. Yet deep inside, something insisted I couldn't stay where I was. While others my age were finishing college, I was only just finishing high school. Still, I pressed through, earned my diploma, and then enlisted in the United States Army.

That enlistment felt like an Abraham moment— as if God was whispering, "Leave your Ur, and step into the unknown." It wasn't faith built on full understanding, but on the assumption that anything had to be better than where I was.

Even in my immaturity, the Spirit was nudging me forward, showing me that movement was better than stagnation.

My father and brothers tried to talk me out of it with warnings of possible wars, planting seeds of fear and doubt.

But I was determined. They had nothing to offer me that would make me reconsider. I didn't know exactly what I was stepping into, but I knew one thing for certain: anything was better than staying stuck.

On the day I was to report to boot camp, my mother was in the hospital undergoing surgery. Before heading to the airport, I stopped by to see her. It broke my heart to find her hooked up to so many IVs, an oxygen mask covering her face, unable to respond.

I stood over her and cried because I didn't want to see my momma in that condition. I whispered a prayer, kissed her goodbye, and then, with my suitcase in hand, I headed toward the airport to catch my flight to Fort Sill, Oklahoma.

In November of 1981, I arrived in Oklahoma and found myself gathered with dozens of others who had also enlisted, all reporting for boot camp. Some looked nervous, some tried to look tough, and others were just quiet—like me—unsure of what was about to unfold.

We didn't wait long before a hard-faced drill sergeant stormed into view, his voice booming like thunder. He barked orders without hesitation, his presence commanding the whole group. There was no handshake, no welcome speech, no warm introduction—just a sharp reminder that we were no longer in control.

He insisted we load up like cattle onto a bus that would carry us to our destination—Fort Sill Army Base. The ride was quiet except for the low murmur of whispers. Some recruits joked nervously, trying to mask their fear, while others stared out the window, lost in thought. I sat clutching my small bag, wondering what I had gotten myself into.

Inside, I wrestled with questions I couldn't shake: Was this really the right decision? Would I make it through? What if my father and brothers were right about the dangers of war? But beneath all the fear, there was also a flicker of hope—this was a fresh start, a chance to prove I wasn't destined to stay stuck in failure.

As the bus rumbled toward Fort Sill, I realized there was no turning back. My old life was behind me, and whatever waited ahead would test me in ways I could not yet imagine.

At one point, we were greeted by an Army chaplain who welcomed us with a brief speech. His words were simple but carried a sense of calm in the middle of all the shouting and tension. Before he left, he handed each of us—at least those who were willing to accept it—a small New Testament Gideon Bible.

When my turn came, I reached out and accepted it with all my strength, as if I were holding on to a lifeline. That little book became a quiet refuge during training. In rare moments of stillness, I would open its thin pages, read, and sometimes whisper verses aloud to myself.

Even though I didn't fully understand all that I was reading, something in those words anchored me. In the chaos of boot camp, that Gideon Bible reminded me that God had not forgotten me, even when I had nearly forgotten Him.

In the eight weeks of training, I learned a lot, and I was well favored by my drill sergeant. For the first time in a long while, I felt structure, discipline, and a sense of direction beginning to take root in my life.

Around Christmas that year, we were given leave to visit our families. I arrived at the Cleveland airport full of anticipation, only to be disappointed when no one was there to welcome me.

It was the story of my life—hope followed by emptiness. That absence stung deeply. Somehow, I don't remember exactly how, Jo appeared with the baby. Seeing them was a relief and a joy, even though my heart carried the weight of how far I had drifted from being the man I should have been.

During that leave, I also visited Pastor Larry Jackson, once a figure of spiritual stability in my life. By then, he had contracted a dreadful disease, one that was devastating lives across the nation.

The strength and vitality I remembered were fading from him, and though I didn't fully grasp the weight of it at the time, I would later understand that he would not recover. In the years that followed, he would pass away.

That loss left me feeling even more abandoned. I was out there on my own. What I didn't realize then—but would later understand after being filled with the Holy Ghost in Germany—was how significant his presence and influence had been in anchoring my early faith. Assumption told me I was alone; the Spirit would later show me I was never truly forsaken.

Reflective Questions:

1. Have I ever mistaken a fresh start or new structure (school, career, military, etc.) for true direction, only to find myself still empty inside?

2. In what ways has God placed "lifelines" (like the Gideon Bible) in my path during times of chaos or confusion?

3. How do I respond when those I look up to—parents, mentors, spiritual leaders—cannot or do not provide the guidance I need?

4. Where in my life have I believed the lie that I was all alone, when in truth God was still present?

5. What "assumptions" am I holding onto right now that may be keeping me from fully trusting the Spirit's guidance?

Reflective Summary:

Chapter 4 reminds us that without the Spirit, direction quickly becomes assumption.

Joel's story of enlistment, discipline, and disappointment mirrors the journey of many who seek identity and purpose in the structures of this world but come up short.

The Gideon Bible in his hands symbolized the truth that even when we nearly forget God, He has not forgotten us.

Family absence, the loss of mentors, and the loneliness of transition can tempt us to believe we are abandoned, but the Spirit whispers otherwise.

What feels like emptiness can actually be preparation—God using even pain and loss to set the stage for a deeper encounter with His presence.

Prayer for Guidance and Maturity

Heavenly Father,

I thank You that even in seasons of confusion, loss, and disappointment, You are still present.

Forgive me for the times I have leaned on my own assumptions rather than listening to Your Spirit.

Teach me to see structure and discipline as tools You can use, but never as substitutes for Your presence. Heal the wounds of abandonment and fill the empty places in my heart with the assurance of Your love.

Guide me into maturity, Lord. Help me to move beyond assumptions, beyond shallow hope, and into a deeper trust in Your Spirit.

When I feel overlooked, remind me that I am chosen. When I feel alone, remind me that You will never leave me nor forsake me.

Anchor my life in Your Word, and direct my steps by the leading of Your Spirit.

In Jesus' name, Amen.

"And in this season, I was Learning to Walk by Faith: Not by Assumption, But by the Spirit."

Chapter 5: Orders, but No Compass

"For to be carnally minded is death; but to be spiritually minded is life and peace."

— **Romans 8:6 (KJV)**

After completing basic training and advanced individual training, I received orders for my first duty station at Yuma Proving Grounds, Arizona, as a Private / E1.

I did not understand that I was the lowest man on the totem pole. If there was a job or assignment that needed to be done that nobody else wanted, they would call on Private Latimore to do it.

However, the military had a way of making a person feel wanted and valued. In the military, everyone knew their places and acted as a team.

Yet outside of that structure, when the day's duties ended, I was left alone with myself, trying to find something to keep me busy.

So, I started drinking, sometimes smoking, and hanging out with the fellows just to fit in. Yes, I was having fun—but in that fun, I began to forget my responsibilities as a father.

What should have been on my mind was what God expected of me. But God was not in my every thought at the moment—only having fun.

As the old saying goes, *idle hands are the devil's workshop,* and mine were no exception.

The desert was dry and unfamiliar. The heat pressed down during the day, and the silence of the nights made me think more deeply about Jo and the baby. It was my first time living on the other side of the country, far from everything and everyone I knew.

It hurts me to even think about how immature and blind I was in those days. But what could you expect from a young man who had never been *affirmed, encouraged, celebrated, or recognized*—always overlooked, misguided, and left without direction?

Because of this, I assumed everybody else was more intelligent than I was, and that insecurity shaped how I thought about myself and the choices I made.

Jo and I wrote letters and spoke on the phone when we could, though many of my calls ended up being charged to her mother's telephone.

Eventually, I received military housing, and Jo and the baby came to live with me. On the outside, it looked like a family trying to come together, but inside things were fragile.

We should have gotten married, but I couldn't bring myself to take that step. My father's influence still weighed heavily in my mind—*his failures, his voice, and his shadow* kept me from moving forward, and I couldn't shake it.

Jo brought with her a lucky talisman that her mother had given her. At the time, I didn't realize the spiritual weight of it, but it wasn't rooted in God, and neither were we.

Still, I allowed it into our home, not understanding how opening the door to demonic spirits would add more confusion to a relationship already under pressure.

The effects showed quickly. We began arguing and fussing over simple things. We both noticed that the baby was having trouble sleeping. I realized that it was a spirit. I even tried fighting it off with a salt remedy I had learned from my mother.

One night as we were sleeping, I saw an image of my Aunt Dorothy pointing to the talisman as the cause of our troubles. I got up, took hold of it, threw it into a garbage can outside of the house, and moved the can away from the house to the curb.

When I came back inside, I saw a dark smoke on the floor. The smoke came alive and lifted itself from the floor to the ceiling and moved out the door with the talisman.

But the damage it had caused—and that we had allowed—was irreparable. The devil was doing his best to keep us away from one another.

To make matters worse, I was unfaithful. I got involved in an affair with a young woman in Yuma, further tearing apart what little stability we had. I tried to juggle Jo and this other relationship, but my immaturity, infidelity, and the spiritual confusion in our home made it nearly impossible to hold things together.

Looking back, I see how broken and vulnerable we both were. Jo was searching for stability in what her mother had passed down, and I was searching for validation in all the wrong places.

Neither of us was seeking God, and without Him at the center, our house was built on sand, not on the Rock.

Unfortunately, Jo and the baby eventually moved back to Rochester. What I thought was just another Army assignment was really the beginning of God positioning me for transformation.

The desert was not just a place on the map—it was the stage where God would begin stripping me of assumptions and preparing me to hear His Spirit in a new way.

Soon, I would be given new orders—this time across the ocean, to South Korea. And though I was not ready for what awaited me there, God was already preparing the ground.

Reflective Questions:

1. What "idle hands" or distractions in my life have opened doors for the enemy's influence?

2. How has insecurity or a lack of affirmation shaped my choices in relationships, family, or faith?

3. What symbols, habits, or traditions have I allowed into my life that may carry more spiritual weight than I realize?

4. In what ways have I neglected responsibilities God entrusted to me— whether as a parent, spouse, or believer?

5. How can I invite God to rebuild my life on the Rock of His Word instead of the shifting sands of my own decisions?

Reflective Summary:

Chapter 5 reminds us that when God is not at the center of our lives, everything we try to build will eventually crumble.

The military gave me order, structure, and belonging, but outside of that system I was lost, empty, and vulnerable to temptation.

Jo and I tried to form a family, but with the talisman in the home, my unfaithfulness, and the absence of God, we were no match for the enemy's schemes.

The desert became more than just a physical place—it was the setting of my failures and the beginning of God's transformation.

My story shows how the devil works through *distraction, insecurity, and spiritual compromise* to destroy relationships, but it also testifies that God's mercy can take even a barren desert and make it the soil of new beginnings.

Prayer for Broken Families and Relationships

Heavenly Father,

I bring before You every broken family, every strained relationship, and every wounded heart.

Lord, You see the cracks caused by *immaturity, insecurity, and sin.* You see the homes where *arguments rise, where children suffer, and where the enemy has planted confusion.*

Father, we ask that You would remove every talisman, every false source of comfort, every unclean spirit that has taken a foothold. Replace them with Your peace, Your Spirit, and Your Word.

Heal the wounds between husbands and wives, parents and children, friends and loved ones.

Where there has been betrayal, bring forgiveness. Where there has been silence, bring communication. Where there has been weakness, bring strength.

Lord, rebuild what was broken on the foundation of Christ—the solid Rock. *Restore trust, restore intimacy, restore wholeness.*

And for those who feel lost in the desert of their own mistakes, let them know that You have not abandoned them. You are preparing the ground for their transformation.

In Jesus' name we pray, Amen.

Chapter 6: A Foreign Land, A Familiar Battle

"Have not I commanded thee? Be strong and of a good courage; be not afraid, neither be thou dismayed: for the Lord thy God is with thee whithersoever thou goest."

— Joshua 1:9 (KJV)

Wisdom Key: A change in scenery cannot change the heart; it only exposes what was already there.

Orders to a Hardship Tour

When my orders came down for South Korea, I didn't know what to expect. This particular overseas assignment was considered a hardship tour, lasting one year.

The desert of Arizona had already stripped me of comfort and exposed my immaturity, but South Korea would confront me with an entirely different test—one that would reveal just how unprepared and unstable I really was.

I was thousands of miles from home, crossing an ocean into a land whose *language, customs, and culture* were foreign to me. The military sent me there with the same expectation as before: *follow orders, do my job, and adapt.*

Some men became so distracted by all that Korea had to offer that they forgot the wives and children waiting back home. I was no better—I was one of them. Yet for some reason I could not forget Jo.

What both of us should have clung to was the prophecy the Spirit had spoken over us in '80–'81.

What we should have done was remind one another of that word. Only now do I understand why the enemy of my soul fought so fiercely to keep me distracted, drugged up, and drowning in sin—he knew that if I remembered, I might return to God's plan.

The truth was, the military wasn't concerned
with our inner battles or private struggles. Its
only job was manpower—enough bodies to fight
a war.

To those in command we were uniforms to fill
the ranks; to me, I was a young man still trying to
figure out who I was and where God fit into all
of it.

South Korea was alive with noise—markets
bustling, neon lights flashing, soldiers and
civilians moving to a rhythm I'd never known.

But in the middle of that movement, I felt the
same stillness I'd felt in the desert: a loneliness
no crowd could erase.

The village knew how to mask that ache. *Booze, drugs, clubs, food, women*—everything was within reach and offered without apology.

Payday weekends emptied the barracks; men rushed out to chase temporary highs that promised to erase the weight of homesickness.

Letters from loved ones sat unopened while new *"companionship"* was sought in dimly lit clubs.

And if a soldier didn't have the money to indulge, credit was easy. Drink now, pay later. Gamble now, pay later. Sin now, pay later.

What none of us realized was that the bill always came due—and the cost was far greater than dollars and cents. We thought we were just having fun, blowing off steam, or easing the loneliness. In truth, we were feeding a system built to profit from our weakness.

Without knowing it, we were entangled in organized crime. The mob was making millions off young, naïve soldiers like me—and we didn't see it. We were pawns in a game we never questioned, blinded by the thrill of the moment and ignorant of the price we would one day pay.

What looked like freedom on the surface was bondage. The more a man indulged, the further he drifted from *responsibility, stability, and the voice of God calling him to something greater.*

At first it felt like relief. After final formation the day dissolved into party—cheap drinks, loud music, lights that never quit, and promises that tonight would make everything hurt less. But relief turned to appetite. Alcohol stopped working and drugs moved in. Nights bled into mornings and days lost their edge.

My letters went unanswered. My uniform went unkempt and my appearance slipped. The club sat on my mind; getting there became the plan around which the rest of my life revolved.

I grew careless with duties I'd once done without question. Each indulgence promised escape but only dug a deeper pit. Shame followed me more than peace; the louder the city became, the more distant God felt—until His voice was a whisper I could no longer hear.

One night I came close to dying: so much cocaine that the room tilted, my chest seized, and I couldn't draw a breath, so it seemed.

Fear stripped away every excuse. In that raw, helpless place I prayed—not in bravado, but in naked desperation: *"Please don't let me die. If You spare me, I will never do this again."*

That promise came from a frightened, broken heart bargaining with God. The silence that followed showed me how near I had come to losing everything—*my life, my soul, the family that depended on me.*

Not long after, on another night when I was stumbling drunk, something happened I still cannot fully explain. I remember being unsteady and then sensing human like figures in white around me—faces I couldn't clearly see but a presence that steadied and escorted me back to camp and into the barracks.

Mercy or vision, I don't know; only that I was guided home when I should have fallen. That strange light in the dark began to pull my thoughts back to God.

Addiction convinces you there is always time to quit tomorrow while it tightens its grip today. It starts as a small concession—one more drink, one more night out—and those concessions add up until they rearrange your life.

You schedule everything around the next escape. Reason gives way to compulsion, and the little lies you tell yourself become the scaffolding of a new, ruined identity. I could see the road ahead; I knew it led downward. Still, I kept taking the next step because *"later"* felt safer than the hard work of turning back.

Even as I sank, God's hand kept tugging. A Scripture here, a flash of shame there, small kindnesses that felt like angels—something would remind me I had not been abandoned.

Conviction whispered when I laughed it off; shame rose when I looked in the mirror. I was far from home, but I could not outrun the presence of God or the truth of His Word.

Lessons in Loneliness

In Korea I learned that distance cannot shield you from your struggles. You can run from people, from places, even from your past — but you cannot run from yourself.

More importantly, you cannot run from God. *He pursues, corrects, protects, and waits.* He was still calling me, still reminding me through **Joshua 1:9:** *"Be strong, be courageous. I am with you."*

Just because you forget God does not mean God has forgotten you. His ways are not our ways and His thoughts are higher than ours, but His mercy is forever.

He showed me that He still cared when He answered my desperate prayer and when I felt a protective presence escort me home on nights I should have fallen.

Whether I name that presence angels, mercy, or the encircling love of God, the point remained: God did not abandon me even while I was abandoning myself.

The Cost of My Running — And the Grace of a Process

I also learned the real cost my running created for others. You cannot leave a woman by herself and expect her to wait without consequence—she has needs, responsibilities, and a life that does not pause because you choose to run.

Jo needed more than promises and late-night phone calls; she needed a husband who would stand.

My absence, my shame, my excuses—every one of them left a toll. That truth forced me to reckon, not only with my own soul, but with the real people I was hurting by my choices.

This is part of what I mean when I say *Learning to Walk by Faith, Not by Assumption, but by the Spirit* is a process.

Faith is not an instant feeling or a single moment at the altar. For many of us—especially those who did not grow up in a Christian home, who never learned the *rhythms and the importance* of church and discipline—the road to steady faith is *slow and stubborn*.

We don't always *"get it right"* the first time. We stumble. We run. We stray. But God's work in us is not tied to one moment of emotion; He is the patient finisher. What He begins by His Spirit, He intends to complete.

That does not excuse sin. It does not erase the damage done to others or the consequences we must face.

Repentance must be real, concrete, and costly when necessary: *apology, restitution where possible, changed patterns, accountability.*

But neither should we let shame become the final word. Grace meets us on the road. Grace is the hand that compels us to turn around and the power that helps us to stay turned.

Practically, the process looks like this for a man in my place: *admit the wrong plainly, seek forgiveness from the one you hurt, take responsibility for the consequences, and put safeguards in place so you do not repeat the pattern.*

That might mean returning home if possible; it might mean refusing the next payday binge, seeking counseling for addiction, finding a local church and a sober mentor, and re-anchoring daily life with *Scripture, prayer, and honest community.*

Faith grows by doing—by small, faithful acts repeated over time—rather than by waiting for a feeling to arrive.

Remember too: Not everyone who meets Christ immediately begins walking in perfect holiness.

Some of us come haltingly, like a child learning to walk—falling, getting up, learning balance. The Spirit *teaches, convicts, and renews* over time.

The promise is sure: God who began a good work in you will complete it. That should give us hope without minimizing the work required on our part.

It is a partnership: *we repent and take the next small obedient step; the Spirit changes our heart and gives us the power to continue.*

Finally, keep the people you hurt in your prayers and actions. Rebuilding trust is slow. It will *require patience, consistency, and sacrifice.*

Let your faith be measured by how you make things right and by how you refuse the old, easy escapes that once ruined you. Let the memory of the fall shape you—both as a warning and as a testimony of what God's mercy can restore.

Reflective Questions:

1. Where am I trying to run from pain or shame, and how have my escapes (drink, drugs, sex, busyness) actually made the problem worse?

2. Who have I neglected or hurt by my choices (wife, children, mother, friends, God), and what would it look like to make one small step toward repairing that relationship today?

3. What lies do I tell myself about "tomorrow" and how can I replace one of those lies with a concrete, immediate action (call a mentor, open a letter, skip the bar this weekend)?

4. Who in my life can I invite into honest accountability — someone who will speak truth in love and help keep me from walking back into the same patterns?

5. Which daily spiritual practice (Scripture, prayer, a short confession, Sabbath rest) can I commit to for the next 30 days to begin reclaiming my life?

Reflective Summary:

This chapter shows how a change of place cannot heal a wounded heart. The hardship of an overseas tour exposed long-standing weakness, and the city's comforts became quick fixes that pulled a young man farther from his calling, his family, and his faith.

Yet even in the depth of self-destruction there was mercy: a frightened prayer, an inexplicable escort, and the quiet tug of God that would not let him go.

The cost of compromise was real — lost trust, missed obligations, and an eroded soul — but the story is also about the slow, painful process of **learning to walk by faith rather than assumption:** *admitting failure, facing those we hurt, and taking small, faithful steps back toward God and responsibility.*

Prayer for a Soldier (Man or Woman) Who Has Lost Something Through Foolishness

Lord God, my Father — you who see us in the dark places and who never stop watching over us — I come before You now on behalf of every soldier, brother, and sister who has traded what is precious for cheap relief.

You know the loneliness, the fear, and the shame that drove them to run. Forgive where they have sinned; heal what has been broken. Give them courage to tell the truth, strength to make amends, and the humility to accept help.

Break the chains of addiction, clear the fog of excuses, and bring steady, godly people across their path to hold them accountable.

Restore what can be restored; where full restoration is not possible, bring comfort, provision, and a new purpose.

Remind them, by Your Spirit and by Your Word, that what You begin in a life You are faithful to complete. Help them take the next small, obedient step — today.

In Jesus' name, Amen.

"And in this season, I was Learning to Walk by Faith: Not by Assumption, But by the Spirit."

Chapter 7: When the Inner War Began

"For I know the thoughts that I think toward you, saith the LORD, thoughts of peace, and not of evil, to give you an expected end."

Jeremiah 29:11 (KJV)

Wisdom Key: Sometimes God's loudest rescue comes through the quietest, fiercest love — the hand that will not let you keep destroying yourself.

In late November of '84, I remember hearing the news of a U.S. soldier found in the woods—his head amputated by the North Koreans.

By the time my orders came through for my next duty station, I was a mess. I was a drug addict and a drunk who needed help. Maybe that was why Korea was considered a hardship tour. The truth was, I was sinking into a slow death and didn't even realize it.

I was no longer the boy who had entered the military. I had become an expert in foolishness—drinking, drugs, partying, chasing anything I thought made me a man. But I was not the man God wanted me to be.

My next assignment was Walter Reed Army Hospital in Washington, D.C. After a short time at home, I was supposed to report there.

I had one foot out the door and the other still tangled in the habits I'd learned overseas. I told myself I would get right— *"after this last weekend,"* I said—but I carried the familiar weight of shame and the dull appetite for anything that would quiet the ache.

When I first came home from South Korea, the jet lag was brutal. I collapsed at my mother's house and slept for three straight days. I was selfish, blind to everything around me. My mother cooked a whole chicken, and I ate the entire thing without offering anyone else a piece. That was the state I was in—consumed with myself.

It was my mother who gave me the wake-up call. She remembered that before the Army I hardly drank. One day, while I was on leave, I asked my younger brother to go out with me for a drink. My mother overheard and asked, calmly but firmly, "What else are you doing? Are you on drugs too?"

She didn't yell. She didn't shame. She spoke as a mother who had watched her son slip away and refused to let him vanish without trying everything to stop him. Her words hit me like a slap. I didn't want to disappoint her. In that moment, I saw how far I had fallen. I wanted to stop, but I didn't know how.

A man can be drunk out of his senses and still hear the truth like a hammer. The room went still. Shame shut my mouth. I had no defense against the look on her face—love that would not allow me to stay lost.

That conversation wasn't dramatic. There were no floodlights from heaven, no falling to my knees. Just bluntness and tenderness braided together. It was the first time in a long time someone had looked me in the eye and refused to excuse me for being young, lonely, or misunderstood.

That is the mercy of a parent who won't carry your sin: she forces you to stand, to own the ruin you've made, and to take the first steps out of it.

From that day on, the struggle to change began. It wasn't clean or easy—it came in stops and starts. When I say my mother's wake-up call delivered me from drug addiction *"for the most part,"* I mean it honestly.

The appetite didn't vanish overnight. Old habits still tugged at me in Washington, and there were nights I argued with myself and lost. But something had shifted: I no longer wanted this to be the story I died with.

Going to Walter Reed felt different after that. Washington was a world away from Cleveland. I drove up in a white '77 Cadillac Coupe De Ville, thinking I would stand out. But when I arrived, I quickly realized I was in another league—this was a place where Mercedes and BMWs filled the lots.

In Korea, out in the fields and on the line, I felt needed. The Army demanded bodies, and as long as I showed up and did my part, I had a place.

But at Walter Reed it was different. Men and women carried themselves with confidence, with education, with polish. They weren't just surviving; they were advancing.

At best, I could maintain within my little space— do my job, keep my head down, and hope not to be exposed. It was a far cry from the false security I had known overseas, where distraction masked insecurity.

Here, my insecurities were laid bare. My lack of education, my lack of affirmation, the quiet doubts about who I was—all of it rose to the surface.

That was when a different kind of battle began. Up to that point, my greatest struggles had been outward—drinking, partying, and the habits I had picked up overseas. But at Walter Reed, the battle turned inward. A voice surfaced, quiet but persistent, telling me I was not enough.

I carried scars no one could see. Because I lacked *education, encouragement, and affirmation* from my father, I struggled to see myself as accomplished. Even in uniform, I felt small.

I watched young men my age going to college, pursuing careers, taking advantage of opportunities, while I wrestled to figure out who I was.

I compared their progress to my confusion. They moved forward; I felt stuck. That gap fed shame and insecurity. I wore the uniform of a soldier, but inside I felt like an imposter—*weak, unprepared, and unsure of my worth.* That mental battle made temptation louder and self-discipline harder.

And yet, even as I carried this weight, I also carried a new urgency—not to be a liability, but to be useful. At the hospital, the work demanded a steady hand and a clear head.

I couldn't afford to be the man I had been in Korea. Orders that once felt like a sentence now felt like an opportunity—a place to practice living a different life. And practice I did.

Some days were better than others. Some weeks I failed and had to start again. But the wake-up call from my mother had broken something in me— the lie that I could keep running without ever paying the cost. Her words had put me on notice, and that notice became the first real tool of change.

Still, Walter Reed was a world of its own. It brought me face-to-face with people who were building new lives—*bright, disciplined men and women utilizing the educational opportunities the base and the city offered*. It was a wild season of possibility, and I let myself get carried along with the current.

I met a lovely woman from Bluefield, West Virginia, and married her—Johanna—but I married without a steady footing. I'd grown distracted and unmoored; I no longer reminded myself of the prophecy or of God's plan.

In the fog of that confusion, I turned to Islam for a season, convinced that all beliefs were the same. It was a lie, and I did not see the danger until it was too late. That assumption weakened me, and the very *"Strange Woman"* the Spirit had warned about—Kelly—entered my life.

From that moment, the prophecy was no longer just a warning—it was unfolding before my eyes. But weighed down by drugs, alcohol, Jo's absence, the loss of direction, and the ache of never receiving a father's affirmation, I felt inadequate and blind to what God was showing me.

Reflective Questions:

1. What inner battles have you ignored because the outward struggles seemed more urgent?

2. How have false assumptions about life, faith, or belief systems left you vulnerable to deception?

3. In what ways do you compare yourself to others, and how does that comparison affect your sense of worth and calling?

4. What prophetic words, warnings, or Scriptures has God spoken over your life that you've forgotten or neglected?

5. Who in your life has given you a "wake-up call" like my mother gave me, and how have you responded to it?

Reflective Summary:

The greatest battles are not always fought in open fields or loud conflicts; many times, they are waged in the quiet places of the mind and heart.

Outward failures may draw the most attention, but it is the inward lies — "you are not enough," "all beliefs are the same," "you can run without consequence" — that do the most damage.

At Walter Reed, I began to realize that ignoring the prophecy and entertaining false beliefs had left me vulnerable. It was not just alcohol, drugs, or reckless living I was fighting anymore, but the subtle war for my identity, faith, and purpose.

The truth is that the enemy is always at work, and ignorance of that battle is as dangerous as outright rebellion.

But God, in His mercy, provides wake-up calls through His Word, His Spirit, and even through the voices of those who love us. The question is: will we hear them, or will we keep running?

Prayer

Heavenly Father,

Open my eyes to the battles I cannot see. Deliver me from the lies I have believed and the assumptions that leave me vulnerable to sin and deception.

Help me to remember the words You have spoken over my life and to walk in them with faith and obedience.

Give me courage not to ignore the inner war but to face it with the strength of Your Spirit.

Guard my heart, steady my mind, and lead me into truth so that I may not fall prey to the enemy's traps.

Thank You for the wake-up calls You send, even when they sting. Help me to answer them and rise to the life You have called me to live.

In Jesus' name, Amen.

"And in this season, I was Learning to Walk by Faith: Not by Assumption, But by the Spirit."

What Have I Learned So Far?

"This charge I commit unto thee, son Timothy, according to the prophecies which went before on thee, that thou by them mightest war a good warfare."

— 1 Timothy 1:18 (KJV)

- That the most significant battles are often fought inside, long after the outward battles seem to be over.

- That running from God's plan does not erase the prophecy — it only delays my obedience and deepens the cost.

- That assumptions about faith and belief systems can be deadly; not all roads lead to God.

- That the voice of a mother, a mentor, or a friend can be God's instrument to break deception and call us back to truth.

- That change is rarely instant; it comes in starts and stops, but every small refusal of the old life matters.

- That ignorance of the war going on around me does not excuse me from it — it only leaves me vulnerable.

- That every prophecy is a summons to warfare; to neglect it is to invite defeat.

Chapter 8: A Spirit-Filled Man, A Fatal Choice

"For the lips of a strange woman drop as an honeycomb, and her mouth is smoother than oil: But her end is bitter as wormwood, sharp as a twoedged sword."

— Proverbs 5:3–4 (KJV)

I was not filled with the Spirit, nor did I understand what it meant to live Spirit-led.

At the time of my marriage to Johanna, I was trying to be a Muslim. I thought Islam would give me the structure, discipline, and identity I was missing. But instead of truly submitting to God, I was only putting on an image.

I prayed when others were watching, quoted words I barely understood, and wore the appearance of discipline while my heart was still chasing sin.

The truth is, I led with hypocrisy. I wanted to look strong, but inside I was weak. I wanted to appear committed, but I was double-minded. On the outside, I looked like a man with religion; on the inside, I was unstable, confused, and bound.

Johanna, unlike me, had been raised in a Christian home. She had values and principles that could have steadied me, but instead of honoring her foundation, I dragged her into my storm.

We married in Bluefield, West Virginia, but I carried my hypocrisy and confusion right into that covenant.

I assumed marriage would fix me—that a new wife and a fresh start would silence the unrest in my soul. But without the Spirit, I was still the same broken man, only now covering my emptiness with religion and wounding someone else in the process.

Not long after, I ran into Kelly in the barracks. When I told her I was married, she screamed and cried out, *"Who is going to marry me?"*

Her words pierced me in a way I didn't expect. I wished I had never heard them, because they played on my emotions. Kelly knew my weakness: I wanted to help anyone if I could, but I didn't know how to set boundaries.

The truth, however, was that I was in no position to help anyone. I was lost in a world of confusion, blind to the fact that her cries were only another snare the enemy was using to pull me away from faithfulness.

Looking back, I can see clearly: I could have escaped those traps if I had been faithful to my marriage with Johanna.

She was not the problem, and neither was Kelly. The problem was me. I was lost, bound, and hypocritical—pretending I had answers when I didn't even understand the questions.

My hypocrisy blinded me to the truth that only Christ could transform me. Until then, every attempt to build a life, a relationship, or even a religious identity collapsed under the weight of my brokenness.

Kelly came wrapped in charm but carrying chaos. Before my reassignment to Germany, she became pregnant, unsure of who the father was.

It was a situation I never should have taken on, yet my weakness and confusion pulled me into it.

By the fall or winter of 1985, I was reassigned to Ayers Kaserne in Kirch-Göns, Germany— Headquarters and Headquarters Company, 2/3 Field Artillery. My focus was completely out of order. I should have been thinking about providing for my wife and children, but instead, I was consumed by false religion, drugs, and alcohol and Kelly.

I was already in over my head and didn't know how to get out. Outwardly, I thought I was standing tall, but inwardly, I was slipping fast.

In Germany, I played the happy-go-lucky soldier, pretending everything was fine. The truth was, everything was terrible. *False religion, drugs, alcohol only made me believe otherwise.*

And then came Kelly. She became the turning point, arriving at the very moment I needed to be steady. Instead of remembering the prophecies spoken over me and guarding my heart, I leaned on my own understanding.

What felt right in the moment became the choice that dragged me down.

Germany stripped away my false fronts. The rigid routines, the cold, and the isolation exposed how thin my *"borrowed beliefs"* really were.

What looked like discipline back in the States collapsed under the weight of real life. I wasn't rooted; I was repeating words and wearing labels.

In that confusion, out of fear and pride, I even denied the Lord Jesus Christ. That denial cracked something open in me. A heaviness settled—oppression that clouded my mind and blinded me. Fear, pressure, and darkness closed in, and I could not fight it on my own.

Mercy met me in an unexpected way—a young Christian couple on base. I finally found the courage to say out loud what I was fighting: demons.

They saw what I could not see and didn't hesitate. They prayed in the name of Jesus, taking authority, I didn't yet understand.

As they commanded that spirit to leave, the atmosphere changed. The weight broke, and something inside me gave way. I hit the floor and sobbed until I had no strength left.

What left me that night was more than emotion; it was bondage. And what entered was more than relief; it was peace.

No more heaviness pressing me down. No more oppression clouding my mind and blinding me to the truth. No more fear whispering in the shadows, no more pressure suffocating me, no more darkness choking out the light.

For the first time in a long time, I could breathe. I could see.

I can now honestly say: I was once blind, but now I see. What had kept me bound for years was broken in a moment by the power of Jesus' name.

And in that season, I began to realize one of the most important lessons of faith: *we don't start the walk by guessing—we begin by hearing.*

Faith doesn't begin with assumptions or appearances. It begins when the Shepherd speaks, and His sheep recognize His voice and obey it.

Life as a soldier overseas was noisy, fast, and full of temptation. We worked hard, played harder, and lived far from the watchful eyes of family and church.

Many of us were young, restless, and reckless—trying to fill the emptiness inside with parties, alcohol, women, and whatever else we could grab hold of.

The barracks could be a lonely place after the lights went out, but we masked it with laughter, bravado, and sin.

Yet in the midst of that environment, God began to deal with me. There were moments when His presence broke through the noise—quiet whispers in my spirit saying, *"I love you";* a sudden check in my conscience; or a scripture rising to mind and coming out of my mouth that I hadn't read or thought about and had no known reference to.

It wasn't constant, but it was undeniable. I didn't always know what to call it at the time, but I knew it wasn't me. It was God.

Looking back, I see now that every true journey of faith starts with **God's initiative**.

- Abraham heard God say, *"Go from your country"* **(Genesis 12:1).**

- Moses heard God call his name from the burning bush **(Exodus 3:4).**

- The disciples heard Jesus say, *"Follow Me"* **(Matthew 4:19).**

None of them were acting on assumptions. None of them were chasing personal ambition. They were responding to a voice.

That was the call I began to learn in Germany: faith is not about trying to prove myself strong— it is about learning to hear, and then obey.

The truth is, faith is not instant maturity. It is a walk. We learn it step by step, often stumbling, sometimes hesitating, but always being drawn forward by the Shepherd who calls us.

And the very first step is this: *before we move, we must learn to listen.*

Not long after, the Holy Ghost filled me in a way I had never known—real, undeniable, and transforming. My appetites began to change. I wanted the Word. I wanted the truth. I wanted to obey.

But one obstacle remained—Kelly. Even after all God had done, I made a fatal choice. I ignored the Lord's warnings—both prophetic and practical—and married her.

The Lord had made it clear: she was not good for me; if I married her, I would suffer. She would *lie to me, cheat on me, and steal from me.* And still, I hardened my heart and ignored His voice.

In my blindness, I even took on her child, convincing myself that somehow, I could fix what was broken in me by stepping into this role.

I thought that raising her child would redeem my own failures as a father, but what I saw as redemption was only rebellion against the clear word of God.

What I hoped would heal me only set me up for deeper pain, disappointment, and sorrow.

Instead of being in a stable, God-centered family, that marriage became the hinge on which my life swung downward.

Everything I thought I was gaining was, in reality, being stripped away. The very covenant I entered into outside of God's will became the doorway to years of turmoil and heartbreak.

Looking back now, I can see the mercy hidden in the discipline. God was not trying to destroy me—He was trying to wake me up.

He allowed the consequences of my choices to catch up with me so that I would have to face the bitter fruit of my disobedience.

Kelly's presence in my life was not an accident; it was part of that wake-up call. She became the instrument through which God exposed *my pride, my disobedience, and my stubbornness.*

The years that followed became a long and painful lesson: that walking by faith is not built on good intentions, assumptions, or the influence of others—*it is built on trusting God's Word above all else.*

It is learning to guard prophecy with obedience, not with pride, and to let the Spirit lead instead of my own desires.

Reflective Questions:

1. Have I ever ignored clear warnings from God—through Scripture, prophecy, or wise counsel—and chosen my own way instead?

2. What masks of "religion" or outward appearance have I worn, while my heart remained unchanged?

3. In what ways have I tried to "fix" myself or others, rather than allowing Christ to do the transforming work?

4. How do I respond when the Lord disciplines me—do I see His mercy in the correction, or do I resist?

5. What lessons from past disobedience can I carry forward to guard me from repeating the same mistakes?

Reflective Summary:

Chapter 8 reminds us that religion without relationship leaves the heart empty. I chased rituals and appearances, but without the Spirit of God, I remained broken and bound.

Germany stripped away my false fronts and exposed my need for the real Christ. In His mercy, God met me through a praying couple, delivered me from oppression, and filled me with the Holy Ghost.

Yet even after such grace, I ignored God's prophetic warnings and entered into a marriage that pulled my life downward.

I recall that immediately after the Lord told me what Kelly would do to me if I married her, I assumed I could handle it.

I had never faced real danger, nor had I known persecution of any kind. In my pride, I believed I could endure whatever came. In a sense, I even wanted to go through with it, as if proving myself stronger than the prophecy. What I did not realize was how brutal the outcome would be.

Before the Lord had left off talking with me and vanished, He rendered a verdict that I will never forget: Mercy. That word was both judgment and lifeline. Mercy meant I would suffer the consequences of my disobedience, yet I would not be utterly destroyed.

No sooner had Kelly and I walked away than her words proved the warning true. She began talking about visiting another soldier on base. I froze inside, thinking, What the Lord said has already begun. It was as if God allowed me to taste the prophecy in its first hour, reminding me that His Word never falls to the ground.

But instead of fleeing, I hardened my heart. That single choice marked the beginning of a downward spiral I could not control.

Looking back, I now see that even in my failures, God's discipline was mercy. He allowed me to face the fruit of my disobedience so that I could learn the true meaning of faith: trusting His Word above my feelings, guarding prophecy with obedience, and never confusing outward religion with inner transformation.

.

Prayer

Father, I thank You for Your mercy that follows me even when I fail. Forgive me for the times I ignored Your voice, resisted Your warnings, and leaned on my own understanding.

Thank You for not abandoning me to my sin, but for reaching into my confusion with *truth, deliverance, and the power of the Holy Ghost.*

Lord, help me to walk by faith and not by assumption. Teach me to obey quickly when You speak, to guard the prophetic words over my life, and to trust that Your plans are greater than my own.

Deliver me from the temptation to wear masks or chase appearances, and keep me anchored in Your Spirit.

In Jesus' name, Amen.

"And in this season, I was Learning to Walk by Faith: Not by Assumption, But by the Spirit."

Chapter 9: A New Assignment, the Same Battle

"Be not deceived; God is not mocked: for whatsoever a man soweth, that shall he also reap." — **Galatians 6:7 (KJV)**

Wisdom Key:

Geography changes, but the heart you carry with you remains the same.

Leaving Germany behind, I thought a new duty station would give me a fresh start. I had to leave Kelly and the children in Germany while I received advanced training at Fort Sam Houston in San Antonio for three months.

I didn't trust her to be by herself, but there was nothing I could do about it. And although Fort Sam Houston was a hub for sin and infidelity, I remained faithful.

After my training, the Army reassigned me to Fort Hood, Texas, one of the largest posts in the United States. Everything about it was bigger— the land, the people, the pace of life. But what hadn't changed was me. The same issues that plagued me in Germany—*disobedience, and the lingering consequences of my choice*s—followed me straight into Texas.

As a recently promoted sergeant, I tried to put on the appearance of moving forward, but the reality was different. The lessons God had tried to teach me in Germany were still echoing, and instead of walking in full obedience, I often drifted back into old habits.

On the surface, things seemed stable enough. We had military housing, a dog named Hanna, and Kelly had been honorably discharged from the Army, now serving the army reserve and as a full-time housewife raising our children.

From the outside, it looked like progress, but inside I sensed something was off. There were moments—awkward glances, strange behaviors—that I couldn't quite put my finger on.

One particular incident stay with me, etched into my memory like a scar that never quite fades.

After formation one afternoon, Kelly came to pick me up. I told her to wait a moment because I needed to stop briefly at the First Sergeant's office before we left.

When the First Sergeant stepped out of his office and laid eyes on Kelly, the entire atmosphere shifted. He froze mid-step, as if the sight of her brought back a memory he would rather not revisit.

His eyes narrowed, studying her carefully. With a puzzled and almost troubled look, he finally asked her, *"Don't I know you? Were you stationed at Fort Carson?"*

Kelly smiled casually, as if it were nothing, and answered, *"Yes."*

The First Sergeant didn't pursue the matter. He didn't ask for details, didn't bring up names or dates. Instead, he simply shook his head slowly, almost in disbelief, and walked away.

He said nothing more, but the disgust on his face spoke volumes. His silence carried a weight heavier than words. It was as if he knew something about her that I didn't—and perhaps something I didn't want to know.

I brushed it off outwardly, but inwardly I was shaken. I tried to ignore the warning, but the truth was already pressing against my spirit.

I had no proof, no visible evidence, but something deep inside told me that what I saw in the First Sergeant's reaction was not a coincidence. It was a confirmation.

The Lord had already whispered His warning to me in times past, and now He was giving me another through this unexpected encounter. Still, my stubbornness and my emotions blinded me.

When I went out on training missions in the field, I wrestled with the gnawing uncertainty of what might be happening while I was away. I couldn't account for every moment at home, and the not knowing ate away at me.

My spirit knew—even if my mind tried to suppress it—those seeds of distrust had already been planted. And when seeds are planted, they do not remain dormant; sooner or later, they grow and bring forth fruit, whether good or evil.

Then came 1990, and with it the beginning of the war in Iraq. The whole Army was on edge.

Orders were coming down from Washington, and units across the installation were buzzing with speculation and dread.

Men were preparing themselves, physically and mentally, for deployment into a conflict that had escalated quickly and promised to test every soldier's endurance.

One by one, names were being called, and soldiers were receiving their marching orders to the Middle East. But when my orders came through, they weren't what anyone expected.

Instead of being deployed to the Gulf like so many others, I was assigned to Honolulu, Hawaii.

It didn't take long for the questions to start. Staff Sergeant Shockley, the company medical section platoon sergeant, called me directly.

His voice carried both curiosity and suspicion as he asked, "Latimore, how did you manage to get orders to Honolulu when everyone else is getting sent to war?"

I had no clever answer, no explanation to give him. The truth was beyond human reasoning. All I could say was, *"It's by the grace of God."*

And I meant it. Because I knew, deep down, that God had His hand on me. I wasn't spared because I was better or more deserving than anyone else. I wasn't overlooked because of luck or favoritism in the system. It was grace— undeserved, unearned, sovereign grace.

While others prepared to face the fires of war in the desert, God saw fit to send me to a place of isolation, where He could continue to deal with me, strip me, and prepare me for what lay ahead.

Looking back, I understand it more clearly now. The warnings I ignored, the uneasiness in my spirit, the providential redirection away from the battlefield of Iraq to the island of Hawaii—it was all part of God's plan to save me from destruction, both external and internal.

He was working behind the scenes, even when I didn't recognize His hand. His silence at times was louder than words, and His interventions were undeniable, even if they confused those around me.

In that season, I began to understand something about God's dealings with us. He does not always shout. Sometimes His warnings come through the look on another man's face, a knot in the pit of your stomach, or a whisper in your spirit that won't go away.

Too often, I tried to dismiss those signals as fear or coincidence, but they were the mercy of God reaching for me before the storm broke.

The First Sergeant's disgust, my own uneasiness, the restless nights when I was away in the field— all of it was God's voice saying, "I told you what would happen if you walked down this path." But even as I ignored His counsel, He was still shielding me.

While others were sent into the desert, I was redirected to an island. It wasn't an escape; it was a setup. God was pulling me aside, not to make life easier, but to deal with me more directly.

I learned then that grace doesn't always look like favor in the eyes of men.

Sometimes grace is simply God keeping you alive long enough to hear Him clearly.

Sometimes it's Him pulling you out of the fire before you are consumed.

And sometimes, grace is Him sending you to a place where the noise is stripped away, so you can no longer hide from His voice.

What I couldn't see then, but know now, is that God was both sparing me and confronting me. The path I had chosen carried pain, betrayal, and loss—but His hand was still on me. His mercy refused to let me go, even when my choices tried to.

Looking back, I see it clearly: the same God who whispered in the barracks, who checked my spirit through a stranger's silence, and who rerouted my orders away from war, was guiding me step by step. I didn't deserve it, but He did it anyway. *That is grace.*

Reflective Questions:

1. Have I ever ignored the subtle warnings God placed in front of me—through people, circumstances, or the unrest of my own spirit?

2. How often do I mistake God's silence for His absence, when in fact His silence may be speaking louder than words?

3. Can I look back on times when God redirected my steps—perhaps away from danger or destruction—even when I did not understand why?

4. What seeds of distrust or disobedience have I allowed to take root, and what has been the fruit of those seeds in my life?

5. Do I truly recognize God's grace as more than favor or blessing, but also as His mercy in keeping me alive long enough to hear His voice and change course?

Reflective Summary:

This chapter reminds us that God's dealings are not always dramatic or obvious. Sometimes His warnings come through a look, a word, or an inner check that refuses to let us rest.

In my story, I tried to overlook those signals, but the First Sergeant's silence and the uneasiness in my spirit were confirmations that God was speaking. Even while I ignored His counsel, He still extended grace.

The Gulf War orders revealed that His hand was guiding me, sparing me from destruction and redirecting me to a place where He could deal with me privately.

Grace does not always look like open doors or easy blessings—it is often God protecting us from unseen dangers, or removing us from situations that could consume us.

The lesson is clear: *listen to His warnings, even when they come softly, and never take His grace for granted.*

Prayer

Heavenly Father,

Thank You for the ways You speak to me—
through whispers, through silence, through the
faces and actions of others. Forgive me for the
times I have ignored Your warnings or chosen
my own path over Your voice.

Thank You for Your grace that has spared me,
redirected me, and kept me even when I did not
deserve it.

Help me to recognize Your hand at work in my
life and to trust You when I do not understand
what You are doing. Teach me to walk in
obedience and to honor the mercy You
continually extend to me.

In Jesus' name, Amen.

What Have I Learned So Far?

I have learned that ignoring God's warnings only plants seeds of distrust and pain. Yet even in my disobedience, His grace has been my covering.

The First Sergeant's silence, the unrest in my spirit, and my unexpected reassignment to Honolulu were not coincidences—they were divine interventions.

God's hand was guiding me away from destruction, not because I was worthy, but because He had a plan for my life that went beyond my failures.

What I have learned so far is this: *God's grace is greater than my mistakes, and His mercy refuses to let me go.*

Chapter 10: A Divine Setup in Honolulu

"Be sober, be vigilant; because your adversary the devil, as a roaring lion, walketh about, seeking whom he may devour."

— 1 Peter 5:8

Once again, as I was reassigned to Honolulu, Kelly and the children stayed in Texas so that she could finish her nursing degree.

I was assigned to the 45th Support Group Medical Section. On paper, it looked like just another relocation, but it was far more than that.

Providence often hides itself in routine paperwork. What seemed like a change of duty station was actually a divine setup—God was repositioning my life.

Most soldiers would have celebrated such a move—*tropical paradise, white sand beaches, and crystal-clear waters.* But for me, Hawaii wasn't a vacation. I was spiritually unsettled. By this time,

Isolation in Paradise

The barracks at Schofield were simple and lonely. I wasn't around other believers. I was surrounded by temptation and distraction. Even though I wasn't indulging in overt sin, I wasn't growing either. It was like standing still in the middle of a storm.

Still, God didn't leave me without a witness. I began attending Holy Ghost Corner Church Of God In Christ, pastored by Elder Wayne Penn.

I enjoyed the fellowship and even joined as a member. Yet, my heart was divided. I was trying to be a faithful husband, father, and minister, but the rulers of darkness were relentless.

A Spirit in the Barracks

One evening after work, I returned to my room in the barracks, tired but ready to rest. As soon as I stepped inside, an evil spirit came over my body — the spirit of homosexuality, or what could only be described as a spirit of cross-dressing. It wasn't a thought or imagination; it was real and forceful.

In the spirit, I saw myself dressed as a woman —
wearing a dress, a hat, high heels, and holding a
purse. I knew immediately this was not from
God. It was the enemy trying to pervert my
identity and confuse the purpose God had placed
within me.

I felt the pressure of that demonic presence, but
deep inside, I made a decision: *I will not agree
with this. I refuse to come into agreement with
this spirit.*

I said to myself, *"I will not leave this room
bound by this thing."* Because I did not know
what other spirits it would attract. So, I began to
resist with all the strength that was in me. The
Word of God declares, *"Resist the devil, and he
will flee from you."* That Scripture became my
weapon in that moment.

Cautious, I made my way to the day room and reached for the phone, fumbling as I dialed the only number that came to mind — Elder Jacob.

My voice was weak and hoarse as I said, "Jacob… something's on me."

He didn't hesitate. He didn't ask for an explanation. All he said was, *"Hold on. I'm coming."*

He arrived without fanfare, like a man who had learned to move fast when the Spirit called.

There was no need for prying questions; his face already knew the gravity of the moment. Jacob stood in my little room, laid his hand on my shoulder, and began to pray with the kind of authority that comes from years of walking with God.

He spoke Scripture aloud, rebuked the lie that had settled on me, and called my true identity back into the light. As he prayed, the air in the room seemed to shift — the pressure that had been crouched over me loosened and then lifted. The vision faded. The oppression broke.

But I didn't walk away untouched. The fear had been real, and the memory sat heavy behind my eyes. It was the same type of spiritual assault I'd suffered in Arizona and Germany — the enemy's aim to shame and confuse me hadn't changed.

What Jacob brought wasn't only a removal of the attack; it was *pastoral presence, steadiness,* and *a reminder that I wasn't alone.*

His prayer began the work of stitching me back together, and his refusal to let me stay in the broken place showed me that God used people to stand in the gap.

That night made one thing plain: the enemy still prowled, but God was already sending His people — in this case, one faithful man named Jacob — to meet him and to reclaim what he tried to steal.

The Ghosts of Jo

Even in Hawaii, Jo never left my mind. I still thought about her and the daughter I had lost to another man while stationed in Korea.

I often pictured Jo smiling in the sun, our little girl playing in the sand, laughter echoing by the water. I could see them fitting into the island life with ease.

Though Kelly was my wife, Jo was the one woman I truly loved. That thought haunted me and revealed how broken I really was.

Thanksgiving Betrayal

One Thanksgiving, I returned home to Fort
Hood. We were living in a small three-bedroom
house on base. When I walked into the guest
bedroom, the mattress lay on the floor. Kelly
brushed it off with a lame excuse, but something
wasn't right.

Later, she introduced me to a man she claimed
was *"helping her around the house."* At first, I
thought nothing of it. But as we sat down to eat,
she served him first and me second—as if I were
the guest in my own home. Then she hugged him
around the waist in front of me.

My heart slammed against my ribs. My eyes went wide and my mouth fell open as if the words themselves had been wrenched away.

For a second I couldn't breathe — not from lack of air but from the sudden, cold clarity of the scene before me.

When he pushed me back it wasn't a casual shove; it was a claim — a silent, brutal announcement: *This is my woman.* The gesture carried a hundred things the man didn't need to say. It carried comfort, possession, and a history I had not been invited into.

In that moment everything inside me split. Memory of late nights in the aid station, long flights over water, prayers whispered in lonely barracks — all of it crashed up against the sight of my own wife wrapping her arms around another man as if the years of distance and duty meant nothing.

Shame and anger rose together, hot and raw. My hands wanted to move — to grab, to strike back, to demand an explanation — but my legs felt like they were planted in quicksand. I stood shocked and small, like a soldier caught off guard not on the battlefield but at the doorstep of his own home.

More than the physical humiliation was the sense of betrayal's calculated cruelty. While I had been fighting spiritual battles overseas, someone had been fighting a different war in my household — and winning ground.

That realization cut deeper than any insult. It was not simply that she had been unfaithful; it was that the *intimacy, trust, and safety* I had assumed were being eroded while I was away doing what I thought was duty.

The betrayal felt like a violation not only of marriage, but of the covenant I had trusted to keep me whole.

And yet—somehow—I forgave her. Not because I was strong, or holy, but because grace was already moving in me. The man I used to be would never have forgiven. But this wasn't me— it was God's mercy.

For all the heat of hurt and the image burned behind my eyes, a quiet, stubborn mercy began to loosen the hold of rage.

I was not instantly healed or suddenly wise; I was simply held by a hand I could not yet name, learning that sometimes survival looks like forgiveness first, understanding later.

Kelly Joins Me

Eventually, Kelly and the children moved to Hawaii. By then, she had become a registered nurse. Wanting her to have work lined up, I arranged a position for her in the Emergency Department at Wahiawa General Hospital.

It was the *"responsible"* thing to do, but it didn't heal the breach between us. On paper, her life now had structure. Spiritually, our marriage was broken.

A Hidden Assignment

Looking back, I recognize the pattern. God withdrew me from the desert of war to confront the desert of my own heart. He did not bring me to Hawaii to hide; He brought me here to be found.

There were nights when Scripture rose up in me like unspoken orders: *Be not deceived... Walk in the Spirit... Be strong and of a good courage.* I began walking the barracks grounds in prayer, groaning when I had no words left. In those prayers, God began to anchor me.

Even at work, as I tended to soldiers' wounds, the Lord held up a mirror. "You treat them gently—will you let Me treat you the same?"

Wisdom Key

Sometimes God relocates your body to reposition your heart. Isolation is not punishment; it is preparation.

Closing Reflection

Hawaii wasn't just a reassignment—it was a classroom of obedience, a mirror for my soul, and a stage for warfare.

What I saw as betrayal, God used as preparation. What felt like abandonment, He turned into alignment.

I had been passive in some areas of my life—letting Kelly handle the bills and the day-to-day decisions—but God used that weakness to teach me stewardship and to call me to wake up.

He was pulling me out of darkness and into the marvelous light. The storm was not the end—it was the beginning of something holy.

Reflective Questions:

1. Where in my life have, I allowed distance or distraction to replace presence, and what is one practical step I will take this week to restore it?

2. When betrayal or hurt comes, do I run toward revenge, retreat into silence, or respond in grace—and how can I practice grace without enabling harm?

3. Who are the faithful people God has placed around me to stand in the gap, and how can I invest in those relationships so they can continue to hold me?

4. What small, daily responsibilities (finances, household, conversations with my children) have I neglected, and what will I commit to changing in the next 30 days?

5. In moments of spiritual oppression or confusion, what will be my first response—prayer, Scripture, calling a brother/sister—and how will I make that response automatic?

Reflective Summary:

This season in Honolulu was a divine classroom. On the surface it looked like a paradise reassignment, but underneath God was using *distance, temptation, and unexpected pain to expose weakness and invite growth.*

I learned that relocation does not mean rescue; sometimes God relocates you so He can work on what you could not see at home.

Betrayal and spiritual assault revealed places of cowardice and avoidance inside me, but they also became catalysts for mercy. Forgiveness came not from my strength but from a grace that softened what anger had hardened.

Equally important was the discovery that God works through people. A faithful elder's prayer, a brother's sudden arrival, and the small duties of daily care—these were the tools God used to begin my recovery.

The lessons were practical: take responsibility for the small things, lean into the fellowship God provides, and respond to spiritual attack with immediate prayer and community. The storm did not destroy me; it refined me.

Prayer

Father, I thank You that Your hand is sovereign
even when our hearts are broken. You reposition
us not to punish but to prepare.

Give us healing where betrayal has cut deep,
wisdom where we have been passive, and
courage to take up the simple responsibilities
You've placed before us.

Guard our hearts from shame and confusion;
strengthen us with steady brothers and sisters
who will pray without delay.

Fill us with a grace that forgives and a resolve that acts. Use our broken places to make us whole again, for Your glory and for the good of those You have entrusted to us.

In Jesus' name, Amen.

"And in this season, I was Learning to Walk by Faith: Not by Assumption, But by the Spirit."

What I Have Learned So Far?

I learned that God's reassignments often expose
what I've ignored. I wasn't much of a thinker
then — I let words and slights roll off me and left
the practical work of our household to Kelly,
even the finances.

That passivity looked like peace on the surface
but it was actually avoidance.

Hawaii forced me to face that: grace can forgive
the past, but growth asks for responsibility.

If God has repositioned you, don't use it to hide;
use it to grow. Take up the small, daily duties —
the bills, the conversations, the stewardship —
because these are the training ground for the
greater calling.

Chapter 11 — Called, But Not Forgotten

"For whom the Lord loveth he chasteneth, and scourgeth every son whom he receiveth."

— Hebrews 12:6

There are seasons when God's mercy looks like a breaking. This chapter is the hardest I write: it tells how God allowed me to be broken so He could remake me, and how He used a woman I had tolerated—Kelly—as an instrument in that painful, purifying work.

When Mercy Looks Like Breaking

I had not been a careful steward of my life or my household. I tolerated things I should have resisted. I let words and slights roll off me.

I let Kelly manage the money and the daily affairs, assuming partnership where I had actually relinquished responsibility. In hindsight, that passivity opened the door to damage I could not have imagined.

One morning she said it plainly: *"I want a divorce."* The words landed like a blow. I was stunned—not only by her decision but by the coldness behind it.

When she moved out and I asked about the money we'd saved, she answered, almost laughing, *"What money? You mean the thousands and thousands of dollars I have?"* That moment woke something in me. A prophecy I'd once heard came back like an echo: *she will steal from you, lie to you, and cheat on you.*

A call to the bank confirmed the shock: my name was not on the accounts I had assumed were ours. I had $65.10 in my account. I learned that while I thought we were paying bills together, Kelly had been paying the minimum and diverting funds.

She had lied about her income, too—telling me she made $24,000 when she actually earned far more. The betrayals stacked up—*financial, emotional, and moral.*

Caught With Other Men

My heart's desire was simple and honest: to raise my boys. All I wanted was to be a father to them.

But God had other plans—plans that far exceeded my narrow desires. As the marriage unraveled, I began to catch Kelly in places she should not have been.

There were late nights, unexplained absences, and then the worst of it: I discovered her with other men, including one of the brothers from our church.

The pain of that discovery was not merely personal humiliation; it felt like disrespect. A brother in Christ—someone who should have been a bulwark—had become part of the betrayal.

Those discoveries forced me to reckon not only with her unfaithfulness, but with my own blind spots.

I had tolerated what should have been resisted. I had made assumptions about loyalty and honesty that were not supported by the life I lived with her. The enemy had used my tolerance as an entry point.

A New Assignment and a Greater Storm

Six months before Hurricane Iniki struck, I volunteered as head medic aboard LSV 163. The assignment gave me distance and purpose. I was busy doing what medics do   tending wounds, organizing care, moving supplies. But distance couldn't erase the unraveling at home.

On September 11, 1992, Hurricane Iniki hit Kauai with devastating force. Our ship was sent on a humanitarian mission.

Working amid the wreckage, I saw the destructive hand of the storm and the restorative hand of people helping people.

The hurricane became a mirror for the chaos that had already been at work in my marriage; it also became a furnace in which God began to refine me.

The Courtroom and the Strip-Down

When Kelly moved forward with divorce proceedings, she asked me not to fight. How could I not fight? My heart and my boys were involved. But the courtroom was not kind.

She arrived rehearsed and polished; witnesses came forward with mischaracterizations; church leaders refused to testify on my behalf.

Judges delayed and at times seemed to favor her counsel. The legal system—*cold, procedural, and often unmerciful*—took what it could from me. In the end she left with the children, the money, a share of my retirement, and the public narrative.

In the courthouse hallway she told me, plain as day, *"I am going to turn the boys against you."* She meant it, and she began that work. The stripping was public and brutal. The courts did not see the whole truth; *they saw performance, and performance carried weight.*

Broken, Then Remade

After the ruling I collapsed under the weight of humiliation and loss. My mother came to Hawaii and did what mothers do—she loved me through the worst of it.

But only God could do the deeper work. I repented. I fasted. I prayed with a fierceness I had not known before.

I began to learn what it meant to walk by faith and not by assumption, to listen for the Spirit instead of relying on my instincts or the appearance of things.

I tried to run damage control. I reached out to people I thought might steady the ship, and I tried to repair relationships that mattered.

I attempted to reconcile with Johanna—hoping that old wounds might be mended—but I learned that she had died of cancer.

That grief landed on me like a second blow; reconciliation closed without even a chance.

I tried to reach Jo, to make peace where I could, to stitch together what had been torn, but those doors were shut as well. Each failed attempt left me more hollow than the last.

When Kelly left, she gave no explanation, closure. She walked out with my boys and with the money I had worked for. I was left *mentally, spiritually, and psychologically broken.*

The loneliness was not simply the absence of a person; it was the erosion of the life I had trusted and the collapse of the assumptions I had built my days upon.

In the midst of that collapse, I found myself staring at a new and terrible truth: I had tolerated what I should never have tolerated, and now I must learn the costly work of rebuilding from the ground up.

Yet even in that darkness a new lesson took root: God will sometimes let the frame fall so He can build a stronger house in its place. My heart was broken, yes, but it was also being prepared.

The deliverance God brought was not immediate or painless. He took me to the end of myself. I resigned from the Army after twelve years of service and returned to Cleveland in June 1994—*wounded, shamed, and with a professional photo of me and my boys in my hands because I suspected I might never see them again.*

But God was at work even in the wreckage. The Holy Ghost, though He felt distant at times, remained my Advocate.

In the dark place I began to pray and cry for mercy—for my family, for those who had betrayed me, and for the judges who had ruled against me. Out of the ashes God began to reconstruct me.

How Kelly Became the Vehicle

It is hard to say it plainly, but God used Kelly to break me. Her choices exposed the parts of me that needed pruning: *passivity, misplaced trust, and a reliance on appearances.* She was not God's finest messenger, but He is sovereign even in the brokenness of human hands.

Through the pain she caused, the Lord stripped away things I had clung to—*security, pride, and illusion*—and in their place He began to give me a deeper dependence on Him.

That does not excuse wrongdoing. Kelly's actions were cruel and low down. But God is not limited by human failure. He can take what was meant to destroy and turn it into a means of purification and purpose.

Repentance and Return to Ministry

Repentance became my daily work. **Psalm 124** and **Psalm 66** walked with me like two steady friends—one reminding me of the Lord who pulled me out when the waters rose, the other proving that the God who tests is also the God who brings us out into a wealthy place **(Ps. 66:10–12).**

For a season I made fasting and prayer my rhythm. The cross took on new meaning: Jesus was accused unjustly and "entrusted Himself to Him who judges justly." I learned to do the same—to stop pleading my case before men and to present it before the Lord **(1 Pet. 2:23).**

Yet, for whatever reason, none of my family seemed to notice how depressed and mentally distant I had become after losing my livelihood, my family, and my job. Either they did not see it, or they did not care to.

I walked with my head hanging low, weighed down by grief and shame. And when people did speak to me, it was rarely to encourage me—they almost always sided with Kelly's version of the story.

I felt invisible and unwanted. The only relief I found came in the classroom at college, the sanctuary of church, and in watching Elder Gwendolyn McCurry exercise her gifts of deliverance and healing.

When God began to draw me back toward ministry, it was not quick or glamorous. It was slow by design. I did not run back to a pulpit. I walked carefully—*wounded, uncertain, and still searching for strength.*

Truthfully, I was not ready to minister to anyone. I was the one in need of *counseling, of healing, of restoration.*

In that valley, the Lord led me to the Pentecostal Church of God in Christ in Cleveland—known to many because of Bishop J. Delano Ellis.

But I did not join for notoriety or platform. I joined because Elder Gwendolyn McCurry was there. God had given her a grace for deliverance and healing, and an ear tuned to His voice.

Through her ministry, the Lord steadied me, untangled my soul, and taught me how to walk in freedom without pretending. She did not flatter me; she fought for me in prayer. She did not make me a celebrity; she helped make me a disciple.

Bishop Ellis himself did not permit me to preach yet—and rightly so. I was still being processed.

God's reforming work often comes through the very people who wound us. My return did not look triumphant. I had just lost everything—my children, my job, my dignity, my trust. After twelve years in the military, I had nothing to show for it.

At thirty-four, I was starting over from scratch: first in my father's house, then in my mother's, rebuilding myself through education while faithfully paying child support.

That is what my repentance and return looked like—not a sprint back to the stage, *but a slow, obedient walk with the cross.* I stopped begging men for justice and learned to trust God's timing.

And when He finally set me back in place, He did not return me as the man I had been; He returned me as a servant—willing to tell the truth, willing to pay the cost, and willing to love people the way He had loved me.

Wisdom Keys

- God sometimes allows people into our lives to expose what we must release.

- Walking by faith requires listening to the Spirit and not leaning on appearances or assumptions.

- Forgiveness does not mean enabling abuse; it means releasing the debt and letting God be the judge.

- Trials purify purpose—what the enemy intended for harm God can use for good.

Reflective Questions:

1. Where have I tolerated what should have been resisted?

2. How am I guarding the stewardship God has given me—financially, emotionally, spiritually?

3. In what ways do I default to assumption instead of seeking the Spirit's guidance?

4. Who are the people I will invite into accountability to protect my household?

5. How can I pray for those who have wronged me while holding firm to justice?

Reflective Summary:

This season stripped away the illusions I had built my life upon. The pain of betrayal and the public undoing of my marriage exposed areas I had tolerated—*passivity, misplaced trust, and a reliance on appearances rather than the Spirit.*

God allowed the frame of my life to fall so He could rebuild a stronger foundation: *repentance, stewardship, and a commitment to walk by faith.*

Mercy and consequence walked hand in hand— what was taken in the courts pressed me into deeper dependence on God, and out of that dependence He began to fashion a ministry shaped by scars, honesty, and compassion for others in their own dark places.

Though the wounds were real, the work God did through them proved that nothing wasted in His hands.

Prayer

Father, when the storms strip our lives and the systems of men fail us, let Your mercy be our tutor.

Teach us to walk by Your Spirit, to steward what You've given, and to refuse toleration that destroys.

Heal our wounds, restore our purpose, and use every broken place for Your glory. Give us the courage to forgive where You lead and the wisdom to protect where we must.

In Jesus' name, Amen.

"And in this season, I was Learning to Walk by Faith: Not by Assumption, But by the Spirit."

What I Have Learned So Far?

I learned to stop tolerating what was harmful. I learned that stewardship is spiritual—*guarding money, heart, and household* are part of the calling.

I learned to walk by faith, not by assumption, and to rely on the Spirit's voice above every human testimony.

Most of all, I learned that even when men's courts fail you, God's court keeps record. Mercy may look like suffering, but in the end it produces a man who is usable for God's kingdom.

Chapter 12: Counterfeits of Comfort

"Watch and pray, that ye enter not into temptation: the spirit indeed is willing, but the flesh is weak."

—Matthew 26:41

The Test of the Flesh

I mistook and underestimated my enemy, the devil. I did not fully realize just how ruthless he is. For years I thought the battle was only about endurance—surviving disappointment, betrayal, and loss. But there was another test waiting—the test of the flesh.

Yet the enemy wasn't finished with me. He knew I was rebuilding, and he hated it. I was still spiritually immature and unaware that the war had not ended. Because I was alone and vulnerable, he sent his henchmen to distract me—women who mirrored the very same spirit that had nearly destroyed me before.

I was craving connection, and the enemy offered counterfeits.

Though I was growing academically and regaining some footing, I remained emotionally exposed. I lacked the maturity to recognize that spiritual warfare had shifted battlefields.

Where bullets and betrayal had once been my battleground, the war had now moved inward—to the level of my desires and my need for affection. The devil exploited that aching void, and I let my guard down.

What looked like comfort was, in reality, distraction cloaked in seduction. I was lonely, depressed, and longing for someone to hold and call my own.

The enemy knew my weakness and sent women with the same spirit of manipulation, seduction, and destruction that had already wounded me through Kelly.

These women weren't partners—they were plants. They weren't nurturers—they devoured. They looked like comfort but brought confusion and trouble for my soul.

They sounded like affirmation but spoke lies.
And in my brokenness, I let them in.

Michelle

Michelle came first. She was somewhat kind, engaging, and seemed to appear at the exact moment when my loneliness reached its peak. Her presence felt like a relief after so many empty nights and heavy days. She gave me attention when I was starving for it, and for a while, that attention felt like medicine.

Early in our conversations, Michelle explained to me that she was an ex-crackhead. I did not know the characteristics of a crackhead. However, that admission alone should have ended things before they ever began.

But she also seemed to be trying to piece her life back together. She was easy on the eyes, in college, owned a home, and appeared to be striving for stability.

To someone like me—already in a broken stage of life, vulnerable and looking for company—that picture of progress was enough to keep me from walking away.

But deep down, I never convinced myself—nor could I honestly affirm—that she was God-sent or a blessing in my wilderness. If anything, she was a mirage in the desert of my brokenness.

At that time, I was already sinking into the early stages of depression, still nursing wounds from *betrayal, disappointment, and isolation*. I was doing all I could to keep myself together.

My heart was crying out for God, but my flesh was crying louder for companionship. And when the two voices clashed, I let the louder voice win.

It didn't take long to see that Michelle wasn't pointing me toward Christ—she was pulling me into compromise. What started as harmless conversations soon became detours from prayer.

What felt like comfort in her company quietly replaced my conviction. She became a substitute for the presence of God, and I allowed it because it filled a void.

With her, I learned how dangerously easy it is to exchange prayer for pleasure, conviction for conversation, and holiness for temporary company.

It happens one small decision at a time—choosing her voice over the Spirit's whisper, her attention over God's presence, her affirmation over God's truth. My soul knew it wasn't right, but my flesh was too eager to silence the warnings.

The tragedy wasn't Michelle herself—it was what she represented: my willingness to cling to anyone who seemed to ease the ache of my loneliness, even if it meant drifting further from God.

She wasn't a blessing; she was a counterfeit. And the longer I entertained her presence, the weaker my spiritual defenses became.

Annette

When Michelle faded, I tried to redirect my life.
In time, I enrolled at Meridia Huron School of
Nursing in East Cleveland.

For the first time in years, I felt hopeful. My
grades were strong, my instructors respected me,
and I wanted more than anything to make my
mother proud. I didn't go to nursing school
looking for trouble—I went looking for a future.

That's why what happened with Annette felt so
sinister. She didn't appear because I chased her;
she pursued me.

At first, it was easy to keep my distance. I avoided the corners where she lingered, I changed my path in the hallways, and I kept my head down during clinicals. I was determined not to be drawn into another compromise.

I knew enough to recognize the pattern—how loneliness could be bait—but I was still weak where it counted. I was reeling from the loss of *family, children, job, and trust*. Those losses had hollowed out places in me that no syllabus, no degree, and no lecturer could fill. And in those hollow spaces, the enemy went to work.

The truth hit me slowly and then all at once: I was standing in the enemy's territory. It wasn't marked by smoke or sword—it was a battlefield disguised as a hospital corridor and a classroom.

The enemy had found a new front, and he was using what I craved most—human connection—as his weapon.

Annette was different in temperament—she was silly at times, lighthearted, easy to laugh with—but the enemy used her in the same way he had used Michelle, and the same way he used Kelly.

With Annette, I experienced firsthand the danger of depending on people to soothe wounds only God can heal. I thought I had found stability, but it was only a false refuge. What she offered wasn't stability—it was intimacy that soothed me for a night but stained my soul for a season.

Her persistence looked different once I saw it for what it was. What had seemed like mere attention revealed itself as a tactical snare.

Even then, I never imagined how quickly compromise could creep in. The emotional fatigue of rebuilding made every soft word; every small kindness feel like medicine.

I mistook flirtation for fellowship and attention for healing. The result was predictable and painful: *my focus eroded, my study habits slipped, and the very thing I had leaned on to reform my life began to unravel.*

Looking back, the lesson is clear and brutal: presence in a holy place does not guarantee holiness in the heart.

I was physically in school, but my spirit had not been secured. The devil didn't have to shout—he only needed to offer me what I longed to receive in the wrong form.

I failed not because one woman was stronger than me, but because the wounds I carried made me an easy target.

Even a divine warning came in the early morning hours—a voice declaring, *"To get into heaven, it depends on the condition of your heart. Your heart is black."* Yet instead of heeding the warning, I remained entangled.

In time, my compromise caught up with me, and I failed out of nursing school. Still, even in my foolishness, God was merciful. He delivered me from the snare, and in His providence, my ties with Annette were severed—for good reason, and for my good.

Harriet

Then came Harriet. Outwardly, Harriet offered what looked like balance. She gave me a sense of safety, and for a moment I thought I had found a steady friend.

But safety without sanctification is only a trap dressed in softer clothes.

Harriet did not challenge me to grow or draw me closer to God—she made me comfortable in my weakness. And the enemy knows that comfort in weakness is just as dangerous as open rebellion.

Jo Returns

And then—Jo.

Jo was different. She was not another passing
figure or a fleeting relationship. She was
someone from my past, someone tied to the part
of me that still longed for what was lost.

After more than twenty years of silence, she
reappeared, and with her came memories I
thought were long gone.

She was married at the time, and I had no
intention of separating her from her husband. I
told myself all I wanted was one conversation—
to see her, to sit and talk, to know that she was
alright.

Deep down, I also wanted to share with her the changes God had made in my life, to testify of how He had brought me through years of brokenness, and how, from time to time, I could now hear His voice.

At first, our conversations seemed innocent. We exchanged updates, spoke of where life had taken us, and tried to cover years of distance in a single meeting. But I walked away unsettled. What I thought would bring closure opened doors I wasn't prepared to guard.

I reminded myself that I had strong moral principles and that I was committed to living by them. After all the hell I had endured, I had drawn clear lines and believed those lines were enough to protect me.

But the truth is, principles alone cannot withstand temptation without the constant strength of the Spirit. Morals can give confidence, but they cannot give power.

And beneath my desire to testify of Christ was something far more dangerous: I had once again underestimated the enemy. The devil knew how to cloak temptation in sincerity. He knew how to disguise longing as compassion and how to turn a testimony into a trap.

I thought I was safe because my words carried Scripture and my intentions seemed pure. But what I didn't realize was that the enemy was patient, waiting for me to let my guard down. In my eagerness to share the goodness of God, I left a back door open for the same weakness that had undone me before.

June 2007 – The Visit

When she visited me back in June of 2007, I intended to remain celibate. I even made an agreement with her beforehand that we would not engage in anything sexual.

But temptation is persistent, and when we arrived at the motel room in Columbus, she insisted that we cross that line.

I tried to resist. At one point, I even attempted to secure another room, hoping distance would help me stay strong, but the motel clerk told me the place was fully occupied and no other rooms were available.

In that moment, I knew it was a trap. Yet I was weary—too tired in body and mind and too vulnerable in spirit to fight any longer. So, I gave in to her desire.

The moment I did, I knew I had crossed a line. Still, instead of repenting, I pressed forward, convincing myself that it could still be worked out.

June 2008 – A Marriage in Haste

Prophetic warnings came, but I ignored them. At All Nations Deliverance Ministry, Dr. Gwendolyn McCurry looked at Jo and said plainly, *"This woman is not from God."* Every word she spoke proved true. But instead of fleeing, I once again rationalized.

She did not pressure me to marry her. The truth is, when Jo moved from Rochester to Cleveland, I was the one who acted in haste. Wanting to create what I thought would be a new beginning, I rushed into purchasing a home in the area where we could live together.

I convinced myself it was the right step, but in reality, it was a decision made out of *loneliness, desire, and impulse*—not prayer, not counsel, and not the leading of the Spirit.

At first, it wasn't horrible, but I began to notice a significant difference in how we approached problems and our roles within the relationship.

Jo proved to be stubborn at times and unwilling to listen to sound advice. What I had hoped would be a place of peace gradually became a place of tension.

The atmosphere in the home shifted—what should have been filled with joy began to show signs of contention. Where I longed for partnership, I often encountered friction.

As time went on, Jo's lack of spiritual maturity became more evident. Her words could be sharp, her criticisms frequent, and her attitude dismissive of the faith I was striving to live by.

I had hoped that sharing a home would bring unity and strength, but instead it magnified the differences between us. What I wanted to be a refuge slowly turned into a battlefield.

Looking back, I realize the problem wasn't just the house or even Jo—it was my disobedience. I had ignored prophetic warnings, dismissed the unease in my spirit, and tried to build stability on a shaky foundation. And when the foundation is cracked, the whole house is destined to fall.

April 2017 – The Breaking Point

The marriage was fractured from the start. Jo lacked spiritual maturity, and her spirit was *argumentative, disrespectful, and overly critical.*

When my son and his family entered our lives in 2017, I hoped Jo would join me in standing on faith during his trials. Instead, she resisted.

Even when God miraculously confirmed His word—telling me to retire, then depositing a large deposit into our account to meet every need—Jo dismissed the vision.

She chose work over faith, undermining my role as spiritual head of the home.

The storm never ceased. At one of Dr. McCurry's services, she prophesied again: *"Jo is going to leave you."* Jo denied it, but the word was sure. Less than three days later, she quietly placed the house key on the mantle and left, never to return.

July 2018 – The Final Blow

On July 23, 2018, our divorce was finalized. For me, it was more than the end of a marriage—it was the final blow in my spiritual life.

Years of compromise, ignored warnings, and misplaced hope had brought me to this breaking point. Jo wasn't just a woman from my past—she had become the embodiment of my unfinished battles, the open door I never fully closed, and the test of the flesh I failed again.

Looking back, I see it clearly: Jo was never sent to elevate me—she was sent to distract me. She represented unfinished business in my flesh, not God's promise for my future.

Spiritually, emotionally, and relationally—she was no good for me. Every prophecy, every warning, every sign had been true.

Yet even in that painful chapter, God was faithful. What the enemy meant for evil, God turned for my good.

I walked out of that courthouse not broken as before with Kelly, but blessed. I lost a marriage, but I kept my dignity, my calling, and my faith.

And I learned this truth: the devil is patient, waiting for old wounds to reopen. Jo was the final blow—but not the final word. God still had a plan to restore me.

And because of that, I not only walk in the principles of God's Word, but I also strive to walk circumspectly. To walk in His principles means I know *His commands, His promises, and His truth*. But to walk circumspectly means I apply them with *care, caution, and reverence* in every step I take.

Principles lay the foundation, but circumspection is the watchtower. Together they remind me that the Christian Walk is not a sprint of emotion, but a disciplined journey of obedience.

This has been the lesson of my life: **Learning to Walk by Faith—not by Assumption, but by the Spirit.**

Reflective Questions:

1. Have you ever mistaken counterfeit comfort for God's provision? How did it affect your walk with Him?

2. What subtle tactics does the enemy use in your life to appeal to your loneliness, desires, or need for affirmation?

3. How can you strengthen your spiritual defenses so you are not only walking in principles but also circumspectly?

4. What prophetic warnings or nudges from the Spirit have you ignored in the past, and what did you learn from those experiences?

5. How can you use your story of temptation and restoration to help others who may be caught in similar snares?

Reflective Summary:

In this chapter, the truth is undeniable: the devil often attacks not with swords and bullets but with whispers and substitutes.

Michelle, Annette, Harriet, and Jo each represented a counterfeit form of comfort, strategically designed to exploit loneliness and pain.

Though each relationship began with the promise of relief, they all ended with the same result— *distraction, compromise, and spiritual setback.*

Yet even in failure, God's mercy remained. What the enemy intended as destruction became a lesson in *vigilance, obedience, and faith.*

The final blow with Jo did not destroy me—it refined me. It forced me to learn that principles alone are not enough; I must walk circumspectly, alert and careful, guided daily by the Spirit of God.

For the last eight years, I have walked this path of singleness—not as a curse, but as a season of strength.

This time has not been wasted. God has allowed me to pour into the community and the church, to encourage others who are broken, and to testify of His grace.

What once felt like loss has become an opportunity to serve. My life is proof that restoration does not always look like marriage, but it always looks like purpose.

Prayer

Lord, I thank You for keeping me when I could not keep myself. Thank You for exposing the counterfeits and preserving me through every test of the flesh.

Strengthen me to walk not only in the knowledge of Your Word, but in careful obedience to it.

Guard my heart against loneliness that leads to compromise, and fill me with a greater hunger for Your presence above all else.

Use my story to help others recognize the traps of the enemy and choose You instead. Let my singleness be fruitful, my testimony be powerful, and my life bring glory to Your name.

In Jesus' name, Amen.

What I Have Learned So Far?

I have learned that the flesh will always seek comfort, but only the Spirit can give true peace.

Every counterfeit I embraced left me emptier, while every time I returned to God, He restored me. Principles give me structure, but walking circumspectly keeps me safe.

I have also learned that singleness is not a sentence—it is an assignment. For eight years, I have lived single, but not idle.

I have given myself to community work, to church service, to encouraging others, and to living out the testimony God has entrusted to me.

In the absence of a spouse, God has filled me with purpose. My life is a witness that the Christian Walk is not about avoiding failure but about learning, rising again, and walking forward in faith.

Epilogue: Not the End, But a Beginning

As I reflect on my journey, I see clearly now what I could not always see then: the hand of God has been on me from the beginning.

Through every detour, every counterfeit, every fall, and every rising again, He has proven faithful. What the enemy meant for destruction, God has turned into *wisdom, testimony, and purpose.*

For the past eight years, I have lived in singleness. At first, it felt like loss, but in time, I discovered it was preparation.

God was not punishing me—He was preserving me. This season has allowed me to walk in greater focus, to heal without distraction, and to pour myself into serving others.

I have given my time to the community, lending a hand where hope seemed thin. I have served in the church, encouraging those who struggle, praying with those who feel forgotten, and teaching those who desire to grow.

I have spoken into the lives of young men and women, warning them of the enemy's traps, and reminding them that God's grace is still greater than their failures.

Singleness has not been a prison—it has been a pulpit. From this place, I have learned to stand strong, to live holy, and to walk with God in deeper intimacy. My story is not about being perfect; it is about being preserved.

This book is not the end of my journey, but the beginning of a new chapter in God's plan.

If my testimony has shown you anything, I pray it is this: no matter how many times you stumble, God's mercy is greater. No matter how cunning the enemy, God's Spirit is stronger. And no matter how many counterfeits come your way, Christ remains the only true comfort.

So, I press on—single, yet not alone; scarred, yet not broken; tested, yet not defeated. I walk by faith, not by assumption, but by the Spirit. And my prayer is that you will do the same.

That has been the lesson of my life, and it is the heartbeat of this book. This is my testimony: **Learning to Walk by Faith: Not by Assumption, But by the Spirit.** And it is my prayer that this becomes your testimony too.

About the Author

Eld Joel Latimore Jr. is a U.S. Army Veteran, minister, and author whose life and writings testify to the grace and power of God. Born and raised in Cleveland, Ohio, he has endured battles both external and internal—military service overseas, seasons of brokenness, spiritual warfare, and the painful lessons of relationships that tested his faith.

Through it all, he has learned that true strength is not found in the flesh but in walking by the Spirit of God.

Elder Latimore's ministry extends beyond the pulpit. For years, he has served faithfully in the church and in his community, mentoring, encouraging, and lifting up those who feel forgotten.

His testimony has become a beacon of hope, especially for those who are wrestling with loneliness, disappointment, and the subtle counterfeits of comfort that the enemy sends.

As an author, Elder Latimore has written works that challenge, inspire, and equip believers to grow in holiness, faith, and spiritual maturity.

His books include **Faith and Fire**: *Walking with the Holy Ghost*, **Not This Woman**: *Delilah's Spirit, the Strange Woman, and the Cost of Compromise*, and **Black People, the Church, and the Reality of the Holy Ghost.**

Today, Elder Latimore continues to walk faithfully in singleness, living out his testimony that God's grace is sufficient and His Spirit is enough.

His life and writings echo the central message that has carried him through every storm: **Learning to Walk by Faith: Not by Assumption, But by the Spirit.**

Other Books by Eld Joel Latimore Jr.

Faith and Fire: Walking with the Holy Ghost

A powerful testimony of deliverance, transformation, and the guiding presence of the Holy Ghost.

Not This Woman: Delilah's Spirit, the Strange Woman, and the Cost of Compromise

A prophetic warning about spiritual deception and the destructive spirit of seduction in the last days.

Black People, the Church, and the Reality of the Holy Ghost

A bold and urgent call for revival, healing, and restoration within the Black community and the church.

The Dream Lives On: A Journey Through Fire, Faith, and the Fulfillment of God's Call

A study of Joseph's life, showing how God refines His people through trials to prepare them for destiny.

Let Us Not Make the Same Mistake: A Call to Spiritual Maturity in the Last Days

A teaching and exhortation urging believers to learn from the failures of Israel and the early church to walk faithfully in obedience.

Back Cover Blurb

Learning to Walk by Faith: Not by Assumption,
But by the Spirit is the unflinching testimony of
Eld Joel Latimore Jr.—a soldier, minister, and
servant who discovered that the hardest battles
aren't always fought with bullets, but with
desires, loneliness, and the counterfeits of
comfort the enemy sends in our weakest
moments.

From heartbreak to hospital corridors, from
prophetic warnings ignored to a marriage that
became the "final blow," Elder Latimore traces
how the war moved inward—and how God's
mercy met him there.

With raw honesty and pastoral wisdom, he names the traps (attention that feels like medicine, intimacy that stains a season, "safety" without sanctification) and points to the only real refuge: the presence of God.

This is more than a memoir; it's a guide for discernment. You'll learn to tell comfort from counterfeit, principles from presumption, and emotion from the leading of the Holy Spirit.

Each chapter closes with reflection, questions, and prayer to help you walk circumspectly in your own story.

Eight years of singleness did not sideline him—it refined him. Today, Elder Latimore serves his church and community with a steady hand, teaching others to heed God's voice and live whole.

If you've ever craved connection more than Christ—or mistaken relief for restoration—this book will help you rise, return, and walk by faith, not by assumption, but by the Spirit.